THE **TESTING** SERIES

TRAIN DRIVER
TESTS

*Sample test questions for Concentration Tests,
Assessing Information, Checking Tests,
Observational Ability, Awareness and Recognition
Tests, and Situational Judgement Tests.*

THE **TESTING** SERIES
expert advice on interview preparation

how2become

Orders: Please contact How2become Ltd,
Suite 2, 50 Churchill Square Business Centre, Kings Hill, Kent ME19 4YU.
You can also order via the email address info@how2become.co.uk.

ISBN: 9781910202890

First published in 2015

Typeset for How2become Ltd by Good Golly Design, Canada, goodgolly.ca.

Printed in Great Britain for How2become Ltd by:
CMP (uk) Limited, Poole, Dorset | www.cmp-uk.com

CONTENTS

WELCOME

Dear Sir/Madam,

Welcome to *Train Driver Tests: Sample test questions for Concentration Tests, Assessing Information, Checking Tests, Observational Ability, Awareness and Recognition Tests, and Situational Judgement Tests.*

The Train Driver selection process is not easy. It is comprehensive, relatively drawn out and highly competitive. In fact, on average there are between 300 and 400 applicants for every vacancy. Coupled with the fact that Train Operating Companies rarely advertise posts, this makes it an even harder job to obtain. However, do not let this put you off as many of the applicants who do apply are grossly under prepared, and they normally fail at the first hurdle.

In addition to this, those people who do make it past the initial application stages usually fail during the Train Driver Tests that form part of the Assessment Centre. This guide will provide you with 100s of practice questions which will allow you to test the same skills and qualities required in the actual Train Driver assessments. Designed by us at How2become we have created tests including: Dots Concentration, Checking Tests, Observational Ability, Awareness and Recognition, and the Situational Judgement Tests. This guide will aid your preparation and improve your overall performance in terms of skills, qualities and requirements for any Train Driver Test.

You must prepare fully if you are to pass the selection process and be offered a position as a Trainee Train Driver. The majority of Train Operating Companies (TOCs) are both professional and meticulous in how they run their assessment centres and you should find the process an enjoyable one. We hope that you enjoy the guide and we wish you all the best in your pursuit of becoming a Train Driver.

If you would like any further assistance with the selection process then we offer the following products and training courses via the website www.how-2become.com:

- Computer based versions of all the Train Driver Tests
- How 2 complete the Train Driver Application Form DVD
- How 2 pass the Train Driver Interview DVD
- Online Train Driver Training Course
- 1 Day intensive Trainee Driver Course

Finally, you won't achieve much in life without hard work, determination and perseverance. Work hard, stay focused and be what you want!

Good luck and best wishes,

The how2become team

The How2become team

PREFACE BY RICHARD MCMUNN

Before I get into the guide and provide you with a host of sample tests, it is important that I explain a little bit about my background and why I am qualified to help you succeed.

I joined the Royal Navy soon after leaving school and spent four fabulous years in the Fleet Air Arm branch onboard HMS Invincible. It had always been my dream to become a Firefighter and I only ever intended staying at the Royal Navy for the minimum amount of time. At the age of 21 I left the Royal Navy and joined Kent Fire and Rescue Service. Over the next 17 years I had an amazing career with a fantastic organisation. During that time I was heavily involved in training and recruitment, often sitting on interview panels and marking application forms for those people who wanted to become Firefighters. I also worked very hard and rose to the rank of Station Manager. I passed numerous assessment centres during my time in the job and I estimate that I was successful at over 95% of interviews I attended.

The reason for my success was not because I am special in anyway, or that I have lots of educational qualifications, because I don't! In the build up to every job application or promotion I always prepared myself thoroughly.

Over the past few years I have taught many people how to pass the selection process for becoming a Trainee Train Driver, both through my Train Driver books, online courses and DVD's, and also during my one day intensive training course at www.traindrivercourse.co.uk. Each and every one of the students who attends my course is determined to pass, and that is what you will need to do too if you are to be successful. As you are probably aware many people want to become Train Drivers. As a result of this, the competition is fierce. However, the vast majority of people who do apply will submit poor application forms or they will do very little to prepare for the assessment centre and the interviews. As a result, they will fail.

The way to pass the selection process is to embark on a comprehensive period of intense preparation. I would urge you to use an action plan during your preparation. This will allow you to focus your mind on exactly what you need to do in order to pass. For example, if it has been many years since you last attended an interview, then you will probably have a lot of work to do in this area. If it has been many years since you last sat a test, then you may have to work very hard in order to pass the psychometric tests that form part of the assessment centre. The point I am making here, is that it is within your power to improve on your weak areas. If you use an action plan then you are far more likely to achieve your goals.

I use action plans in just about every element of my work. Action plans work simply because they focus your mind on what needs to be done. Once you have created your action plan, stick it in a prominent position such as your fridge door. This will act as a reminder of the work that you need to do in order to prepare properly for selection. Your action plan might look something like this:

My weekly action plan for preparing for Train Driver selection

Monday	Tuesday	Wednesday	Thursday	Friday
Research into the TOC I am applying for. Includes reading recruitment literature and visiting websites.	60 minute Interview preparation including preparing my responses to questions.	Obtain application form and read recruitment literature and application form guidance notes.	Research into the TOC I am applying for. Includes reading recruitment literature and visiting websites.	60 minute mock interview with a friend or relative.
60 minutes preparation on Mechanical Comprehension tests and Checking Tests.	30 minute Dots Concentration Test preparation.	45 minute fast reaction preparation using 'Bop it' toy.	'60 minutes preparation on Mechanical Comprehension tests and Checking Tests.	30 minute Dots Concentration Test preparation.

Monday	Tuesday	Wednesday	Thursday	Friday
20 minute jog or brisk walk.	30 minutes gym work.	20 minutes reading about the role of a Train Driver.	20 minute jog or brisk walk.	30 minutes gym work.

Note: Saturday and Sunday, rest days.

The above sample action plan is just a simple example of what you may wish to include. Your action plan will very much depend on your strengths and weaknesses.

Areas that you may wish to include in your action plan could be:

- Researching the role of a Train Driver;

- Researching the training that you will undergo as a Trainee Train Driver;

- Researching the Train Operating Company that you are applying for;

- Dedicating time to completing the application form and reading the guidance notes;

- Carrying out practice tests that are similar to the ones required at the assessment centre;

- Light fitness work in order to keep up your concentration levels;

- Interview preparation including carrying out a mock interview.

During my career I have been successful at over 95% of interviews and assessments that I've attended. The reason for this is simply because I always embark on a period of focused preparation, and I always aim to improve on my weak areas. Follow this simple process and you too can enjoy the same levels of success that I have enjoyed.

Finally, it is very important that you believe in your own abilities. It does not matter if you have no qualifications. It does not matter if you have no knowledge yet of the role of a Train Driver. What does matter is self belief, self discipline and a genuine desire to improve and become successful.

Best wishes,

Richard McMunn

Richard McMunn

CHAPTER ONE
ASSESSING INFORMATION TEST

Train Drivers have to undertake tests that focus on their abilities and skills that are essential for any a job position as a Train Driver. During this chapter, we have created a test called Assessing Information that will ultimately help you prepare for your real assessment.

Whilst we cannot stress enough that this test is not a real test, and that we have no link to the Train Operating Companies who conduct your assessments, these tests should only be used as a guideline tool, in order to improve the key skills and requirements, they should not be used as an indication of actual Train Driver assessments.

During this practice test, you will be given a large set of information for which you need to memorise. You are advised to take notes, and should time yourself using the time frame of approximately 4 minutes to read the passage. Then, once those 4 minutes are up you should begin to answer the following questions in relation to that passage.

This practice test not only allows you to work on your memory skills, and recall information in a certain amount of time, it also allows you to work on your timing and concentration skills.

Primarily this test is designed by us at How2become to help prepare you for the difficult selection process of becoming a Train Driver. We have done our utmost to ensure you with the best preparation guide that will allow you to increase your overall chances of successfully completing the selection process.

TEST 1, SECTION 1

You have 4 minutes only to read the following passage and take notes before answering the questions on the following page.

Train tracks are made up of three main components: the metal rails, the sleepers that sit firmly underneath the rails and the ballast – the crushed rock segments that form a bed for the tracks to lie in.

A tamping machine, or a ballast tamper, is a machine that can be used for raising, straightening and altering the tracks. It is a machine that compresses the track ballast (the crushed segments of rock) under the rail track in order to make it more durable. Originally, this work was done manually, whereby labourers would use beaters as a way of pressing down the rock. Despite being faster, more accurate, efficient and less intensive, tamping machines are essential for the production and usage of creating stable tracks from concentre, typically weighing 250 kg.

For train tracks to work efficiently, the alignment of the tracks must be seam-less. The sleepers that sit firmly underneath the rails, must also sit firmly in the crushed rock. If a track has been used for many years, or changes to the track have been made, the alignment of all three components needs to be altered in order to remain stable and effective. The gaps in the underlying rock bed need to be filled so that the sleepers do not move as a train passes along. This allows the train to run smoothly and ultimately reduces noise, vibrations and more importantly, any hazards.

Tamping machines can be used to fix these gaps by placing them on the track. It then conducts vibrations with hydraulic 'fingers' to remove all the gaps in the ballast, and align the track up. These machines are very noisy and often cause disruption. Not only are the machines themselves noisy, but they also trigger track alarms which act as a warning sign for workers of ap-proaching trains.

Most tamping jobs are conducted during the night, in order to avoid disrupt-ing train services. By conducting this job at night, therefore can affect nearby neighbourhoods for one or two nights. Due to tamping machines being a part of regular maintenance work, Train Operating Companies are often un-able to notify neighbourhoods that may be disturbed.

Question 1

Name **one** component that makes up the train tracks. Three **possible** answers.

Answer [   ]

Question 2

What is the name of the machine that is used in order to compress the crushed rock underneath the rail tracks?

A – Tampering machine

B – Tangent machine

C – Hydraulics machine

D – Tamping machine

E – Tramping machine

Answer [   ]

Question 3

What is the typical weight of the concrete used in the production process?

A – 150 kg

B – 200 kg

C – 250 kg

D – 300 kg

E – 350 kg

Answer [   ]

Question 4

The machine compresses the rock underneath the tracks, in order to make the tracks more....

A – Flexible

B – Diverse

C – Tangent

D – Resistant

E – Durable

Answer

Question 5

Whereabouts are the sleepers positioned?

A – Underneath the ballast

B – To the side of the ballast

C – Underneath the rails

D – To the side of the rails

E – On top of the rails

Answer

Question 6

What is the main job of the machine?

A – To compress the rock

B – To align the rails

C – To generate vibrations

D – To assist the trains mobility

E – To fix any gaps and voids in the track alignment

Answer

Question 7

What does these machines often trigger?

A – Signals

B – Mobility

C – Light

D – Alarms

E – Cannot be determined

Answer

Question 8

The alarms have been triggered. What is the reason for the alarm?

A – The sound of the job completed

B – To warn workers of an approaching train

C – The sound of the job beginning

D – The warn neighbours of work in progress

E – Cannot be determined

Answer

Question 9

What time, day or night, are tamping machines often used?

Answer

Question 10

What does this machinery conduct? **Two** answers needed.

A – Heat

B – Vibrations

C – Light

D – Noise

E – Mobility

Answer [ ]

Question 11

How was this job done originally?

Answer [ ]

Question 12

How often are the neighbourhoods living close by, notified of work with these machines?

A – Very often

B – Often

C – Neutral

D – Hardly ever

E – Never

Answer [ ]

Question 13

What is another name of the type of machine used?

Answer [ ]

Question 14

Why might the train track have gaps in the ballast?

A – Animals digging holes underneath the train tracks

B – The rock has eroded

C – The tracks have been used for many years

D – The infrastructure was not made correctly

E – Cannot be determined

Answer

ANSWERS TO TEST 1, SECTION 1

Q1. Metal rails, the sleepers or the ballast – you are only asked for one answer, and so any of these answers will be correct.

Q2. D = tamping machine

Q3. C = 250 kg

Q4. E = durable

Q5. C = underneath the rails

Q6. E = to fix any gap or void in the track alignment

Q7. D = alarms

Q8. B = to warn workers of an approaching train

Q9. Night

Q10. B = vibrations and D = noise

Q11. Manually, with the use of beaters

Q12. D = hardly ever

Q13. Ballast tamper

Q14. C = has been used for many years

TEST 1, SECTION 2

You have 4 minutes only to read the following passage and take notes before answering the questions on the following page.

Freight trains are primarily used to transport cargo and goods, as opposed to transporting passengers. The railway network in Great Britain has been used to transport goods of various types and in various contingencies since the early 19th century. Whilst good traffic in the UK is considerably lower than other countries, it continues to be used, and continues to grow.

Rail freight has become extremely vital in regards to Britain's economic success. It is argued that using rail freight has contributed to over £800 million to the economy. Not only that, but it has also reduced congestion and carbon emissions, and therefore making this use of transportation more environmentally friendly.

Whether it is transporting raw materials for manufacturing purposes, fuels for electrical generations or consumer goods, businesses in the UK rely on freight trains to transport the cargo in an environmentally friendly and efficient way.

The UK has become more reliant on the use of rail freight which provides a faster, safer, greener and efficient way of transporting loads of cargo. It has been said that rail freight is expected to grow in demand by 30% in the next decade. This is equivalent to 240 additional freight trains per day.

In order to maintain and uphold this level of continual growth and demand for freight trains, train operating companies will work in partnership with the government to move cargo transports off of the road, and improve the quality of life by substantially reducing carbon emissions.

It is fact that, on average, a gallon of fuel will move a tonne of goods 246 miles on rail, but only 88 miles by road. Also, each freight train that is used, takes 60 HGV lorries off the road, ultimately helping carbon emissions.

During the First World War, it was renowned as the "Railway War". Thousands of tonnes of supplies and munitions were distributed all over Great Britain, whereby the supplies were dispatched from ports in the South East to be shipped over to France and the Front Line. A number of programmes were instigated in order for railways to meet the huge demands of the wartime. The Common User Agreement, conducted under the Coal Transport Act of 1917 are two examples of programmes that ultimately enabled better railway services. Over 100 train operating companies collaborated on these programmes and worked together in aid of national interest.

Question 1

What do freight trains carry?

A – Passengers

B – Cargo

C – Passengers and cargo

D – Cannot be determined

Answer [   ]

Question 2

How long has freight trains been in use in Great Britain?

A – Early 17th century

B – Late 17th century

C – Early 18th century

D – Late 18th century

E – Early 19th century

Answer [   ]

Question 3

The use of rail freight for Britain has been extremely vital in regards to…

A – Government success

B – Train Operating Companies becoming more popular

C – Economical success

D – Transport safety

E – Cannot be determined

Answer [   ]

Question 4

On average, how much has rail freight contributed to the economy?

A – £600 million

B – £800 million

C – £300 million

D – £500 million

E – £900 million

Answer

Question 5

Which two of the following answers can be concluded from rail freight being more environmentally friendly? **Two** answers required.

A – Reduces carbon emissions

B – Reduces the use of HGV's

C – Reduces cost

D – Reduces congestion

E – Reduces numerous transportation methods

Answer

Question 6

On average, a gallon of fuel for freight trains can move a tonne of goods how far?

A – 88 miles

B – 100 miles

C – 246 miles

D – 276 miles

E – 44 miles

Answer

Question 7

On average, a gallon of fuel for road usage can move a tonne of goods how far?

A – 246 miles

B – 44 miles

C – 102 miles

D – 88 miles

E – 70 miles

Answer

Question 8

If a freight train is used, how many HGV lorries are taken off the road?

A – 40

B – 60

C – 30

D – 70

E – 80

Answer

Question 9

How much are freight trains expected to grow in demand within one decade?

A – 20%

B – 70%

C – 50%

D – 40%

E – 30%

Answer

Question 10

If freight trains continue to grow at the rate that is expected, how many additional freight trains will be used per day?

A – 210

B – 240

C – 200

D – 180

E – 190

Answer

Question 11

How many train companies collaborated on the programmes that were instigated during the First World War?

A – Over 50

B – Over 60

C – Over 20

D – Over 80

E – Over 100

Answer

Question 12

What was the name of the Act that enabled better transport services during World War I?

A – Coal Transport Act 1921

B – Coal Transport Act 1917

C – Coal Transport Act 1912

D – Coal Transport Act 1931

E – Coal Transport Act 1940

Answer

Question 13

What was the First World War also known as?

A – Britain's War

B – British Railway War

C – Front Line War

D – Railway War

E – Cannot be determined

Answer

Question 14

Where were the supplies being shipped? **Two** answers required.

A – Germany

B – France

C – Front Line

D – England

E – Cannot be determined

Answer

ANSWERS TO TEST 1, SECTION 2

Q1. B = cargo

Q2. E = early 19th century

Q3. C = economical success

Q4. B = £800 million

Q5. A = reduces carbon emissions, D = reduces congestion

Q6. C = 246 miles

Q7. D = 88 miles

Q8. B = 60

Q9. E = 30%

Q10. B = 240

Q11. E = over 100

Q12. B = Coal Transport Act 1917

Q13. D = Railway War

Q14. B = France, C = Front Line

TEST 1, SECTION 3

You have 4 minutes only to read the following passage and take notes before answering the questions on the following page.

The railway system of Great Britain is one of the oldest in the world. The first steam locomotive was used in Britain's nation, and is has become a paramount feature of contemporary society.

The arrival of railways has subsequently contributed to the dramatic growth in Industrialisation during the nineteenth century, and has ultimately had profound impacts on social and economical changes. The railway 'filled a void' in what other means of transport could not. Railways were able to provide an efficient, fast, cost effective and environmentally friendly service that catered for the needs of many people.

The history of the railways in Great Britain is remarkable. To see the incredible changes over hundreds of years is remarkable and can only be described as the 'transformation of transport'. In 1804, the first successful steam locomotive runs on wheels, and was used to transport iron across a track of nine miles. Built by Richard Trevithick's, the locomotive – 'the Penydarren', was the World's first steam engine to run on rails.

Since the early 19th century, railways have continued to develop and are now a strong infrastructure within hundreds of societies. During the First World War, the Government took over and run the railways until 1921, when private railway companies regained control. During 1921, an Act was passed in Parliament which submerged four railway companied: known simply as the 'British Rail'.

During 1940 in the Second World War, the companies effectively worked together to help Britain's war efforts, and in the late 1940's, these railways were nationalised and formed the 'British Railways', which was implemented under the Transport Act. In the 50's, society saw a modernised change in regards to railway services. Diesel and electrical trains were introduced and started to replace the steam locomotive trains.

In 1960, the railways were re-organised in hope to make money. Secondary routes and branch lines closed. As rationalisation took hold at this time, one-third of the pre-1948 networks had closed. A giant leap was undertaken in the 70's, and saw the introduction of the 'high-speed diesel-electric' service trains, and by 1990 both main coastal express routes, the East and West

Coast Main Lines had been electrified between central Scotland and London.

In 1994, the Channel Tunnel opened and began the service from England to France. This exponential growth in regards to the railway services has considerably changed over the years, and is believed to continue to adapt.

In 2011, the number of journeys in Great Britain between 2010 and 2011 reaches a record breaking 1.16 billion, and by 2013, the railways are believed to be the second safest in Europe (after Luxembourg), and ultimately delivers a modernised service or both local and national railway routes.

Question 1

Where was the first steam locomotive train used?

A – China

B – Germany

C – France

D – Britain

E – Spain

Answer

Question 2

The railway was able to do what, that other transportation methods could not?

A – Create profits

B – Fill a void

C – Reduce carbon emissions

D – Help Industrialise society

E – Create transport for the middle classes

Answer

Question 3

In what year was the first running steam locomotive train made?

A – 1800

B – 1901

C – 1821

D – 1804

E – 1904

Answer

Question 4

What was the name of the 'mechanical genius' who built the first steam locomotive train?

Answer

Question 5

What was the first steam locomotive train called?

Answer

Question 6

In 1921, the railway service an Act in Parliament was implemented and saw the introduction of...

A – 'British Railways'

B – 'Great British Railways'

C – 'The four rails'

D – 'British Rail'

E – Cannot be determined

Answer

Question 7

What was the name of the Act in 1940 that nationalised the four railways?

A – Transportation Act

B – Local Transport Act

C – Transport Act

D – National Transport Act

E – Cannot be determined

Answer

Question 8

What fraction of the pre-1948 services closed in 1960?

A – One half

B – One quarter

C – One fifth

D – One third

E – Three thirds

Answer [ ]

Question 9

What type of trains were introduced in 1970?

A – High speed

B – Diesel

C – Electrical

D – Steam

E – All of the above

Answer [ ]

Question 10

What opened in 1994?

A – Medway Tunnel

B – Bradway Tunnel

C – The Channel Tunnel

D – Redhill Tunnel

E – Dartford Tunnel

Answer [ ]

Question 11

Between 2010 and 2011, the number of journeys reached a record breaking...

A – 1.61 billion

B – 1.16 billion

C – 1.66 billion

D – 1.16 million

E – 6.16 billion

Answer [   ]

Question 12

What is the safest railway in Europe?

Answer [   ]

Question 13

What service does the Channel Tunnel offer? I.e. England to...?

Answer [   ]

Question 14

In what year did private train companies regain control of the railway services?

A – 1984

B – 1904

C – 1911

D – 1927

E – 1921

Answer [   ]

ANSWERS TO TEST 1, SECTION 3

Q1. D = Britain

Q2. B = fill a void

Q3. D = 1804

Q4. Richard Trevithick

Q5. 'The Penydarren'

Q6. D = British Rail

Q7. C = Transport Act

Q8. D = one third

Q9. A = high speed

Q10. C = the Channel Tunnel

Q11. B = 1.16 billion

Q12. Luxembourg

Q13. France

Q14. E = 1921

CHAPTER TWO
CHECKING TESTS

Another way of preparing for your Train Driver Tests is to practice your skills in relation to checking faults and finding errors from a set of diagrams.

Again, these practice questions should only be used to work on the key skills and qualities required for an aspiring Train Driver. They should not be used in association with the real train driver tests. We have only provided you these question types in order to better your chances and improve on your skills that are essential to successfully pass the selection process.

During this practice test, we have provided a series of diagrams and your task is to work out which order should be checked first. This type of practice test has been specifically designed by us at How2become to allow you to practice prioritising a series of diagrams. This type of task will be essential for any aspiring Train Driver, and so we feel it is beneficial that you practice these types of questions, in order to better your chances overall.

Example

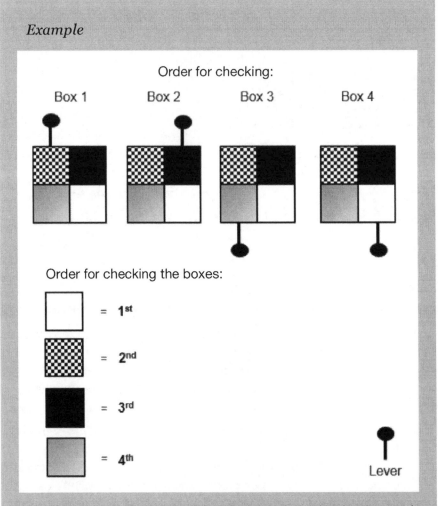

Order for checking:

Box 1   Box 2   Box 3   Box 4

Order for checking the boxes:

☐ = **1ˢᵗ**

▦ = **2ⁿᵈ**

■ = **3ʳᵈ**

▨ = **4ᵗʰ**

Lever

For these types of questions, it is important to take the time and carefully look at the key you are given.

- For the above example, you will notice that box 4 would need to be checked first. This is because the lever has been placed in a white box (which indicates that it needs to be first priority for checking).

- The next box that would need to be checked is box 1, then box 2, and then box 3.

Answer: 4123

CHECKING TESTS – **TEST SECTION 1**

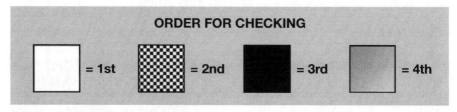

For the following ten questions, write down the order in which the boxes should be checked using the 'Order for Checking' sequence above:

Question 1

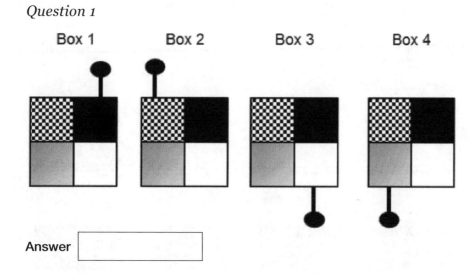

Answer

Question 2

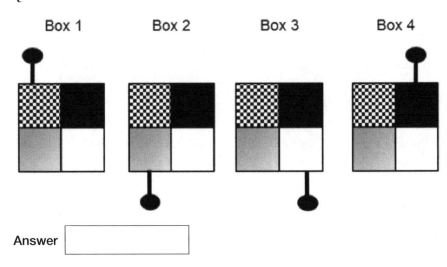

Answer

Question 3

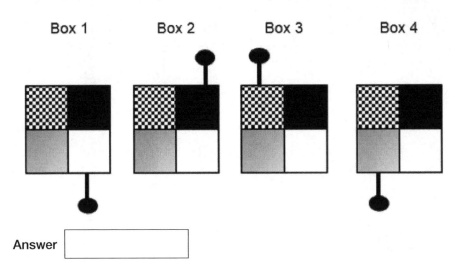

Answer

Question 4

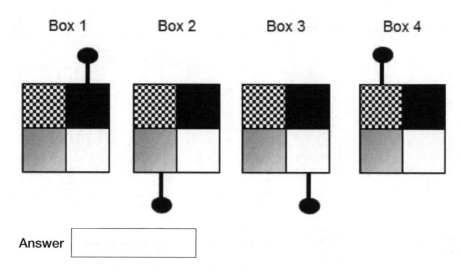

Answer [   ]

Question 5

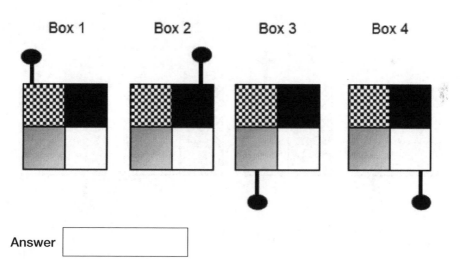

Answer [   ]

Question 6

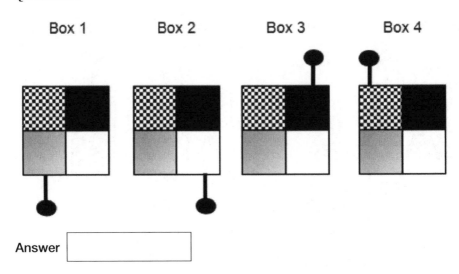

Answer

Question 7

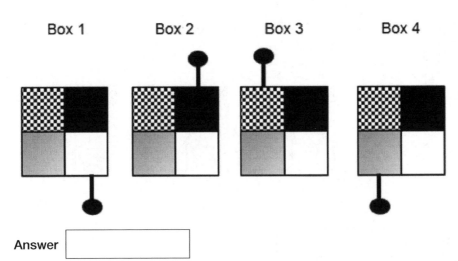

Answer

Question 8

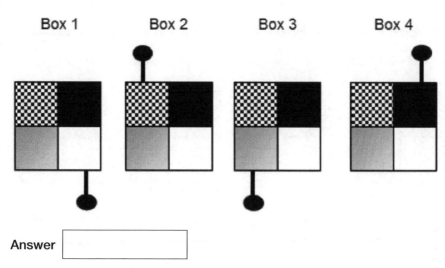

Answer [   ]

Question 9

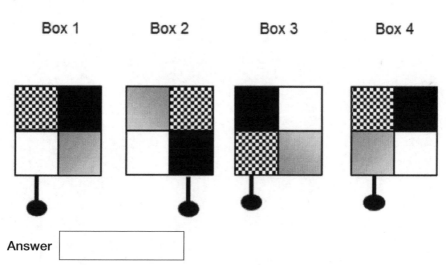

Answer [   ]

Question 10

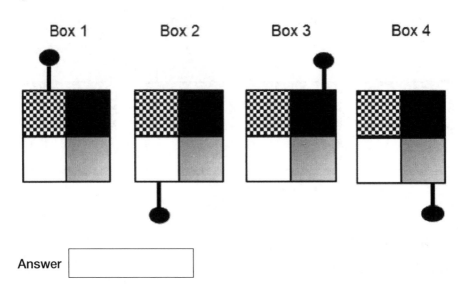

| Box 1 | Box 2 | Box 3 | Box 4 |

Answer

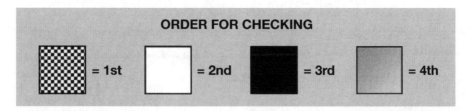

For the following ten questions, write down the order in which the boxes should be checked using the 'Order for Checking' sequence above:

Question 11

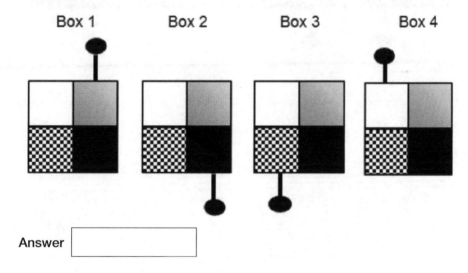

Answer

Question 12

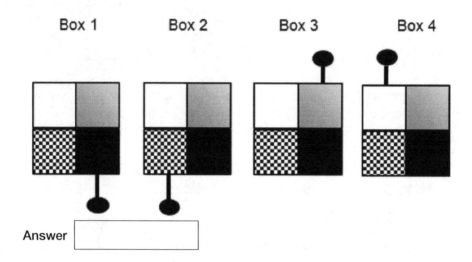

Answer

Question 13

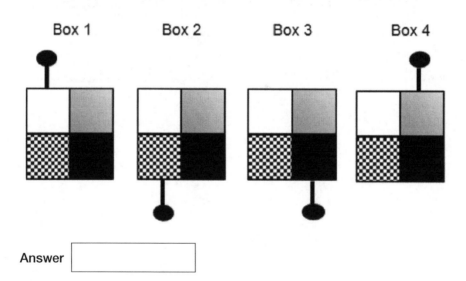

Answer

Question 14

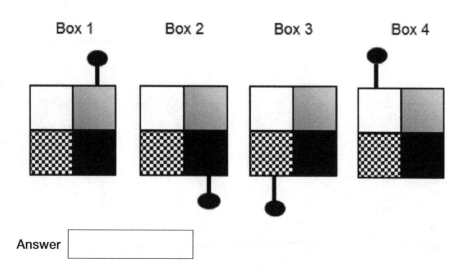

Answer [   ]

Question 15

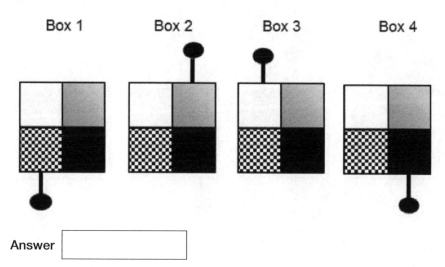

Answer [   ]

Question 16

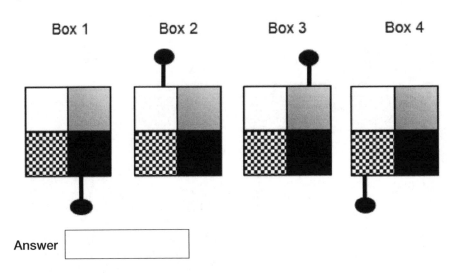

Answer [   ]

Question 17

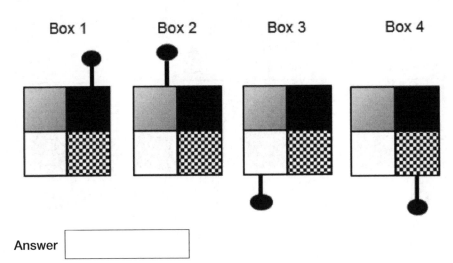

Answer [   ]

Question 18

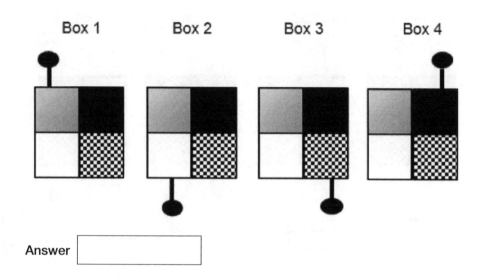

Answer [   ]

Question 19

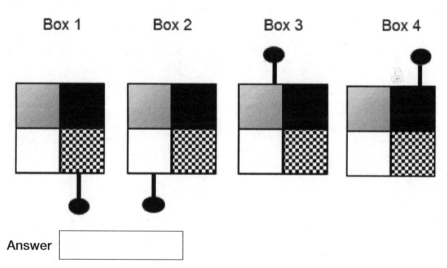

Answer [   ]

Question 20

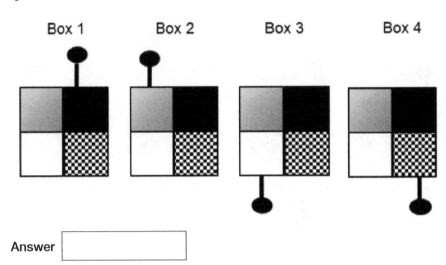

Answer _____

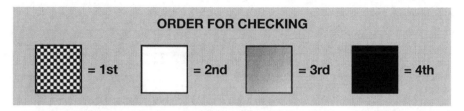

For the following five questions, write down the order in which the boxes should be checked using the 'Order for Checking' sequence above

Question 21

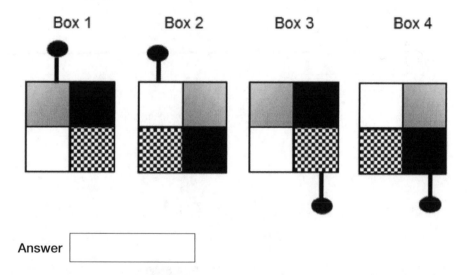

Answer [   ]

Question 22

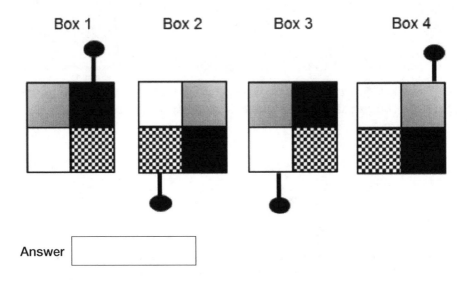

Answer [   ]

Question 23

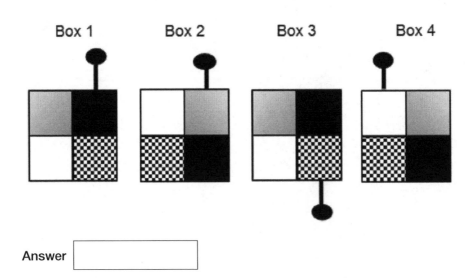

Answer [   ]

Question 24

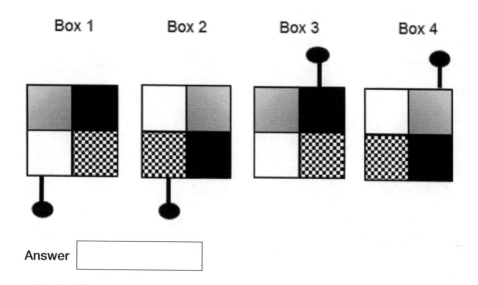

Box 1 Box 2 Box 3 Box 4

Answer

Question 25

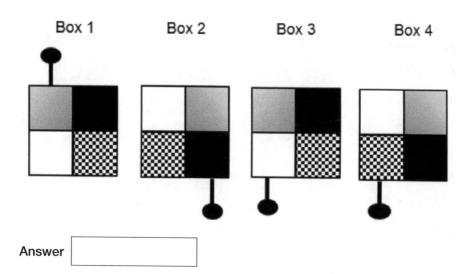

Box 1 Box 2 Box 3 Box 4

Answer

ANSWERS TO CHECKING TESTS - **TEST SECTION 1**

Q1. 3214

Q2. 3142

Q3. 1324

Q4. 3412

Q5. 4123

Q6. 2431

Q7. 1324

Q8. 1243

Q9. 1324

Q10. 2134

Q11. 3421

Q12. 2413

Q13. 2134

Q14. 3421

Q15. 1342

Q16. 4213

Q17. 4312

Q18. 3241

Q19. 1243

Q20. 4312

Q21. 3214

Q22. 2341

Q23. 3421

Q24. 2143

Q25. 4312

CHECKING TESTS – **TEST SECTION 2**

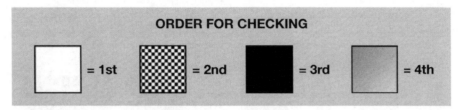

For the following ten questions, write down the order in which the boxes should be checked using the 'Order for Checking' sequence above:

Question 1

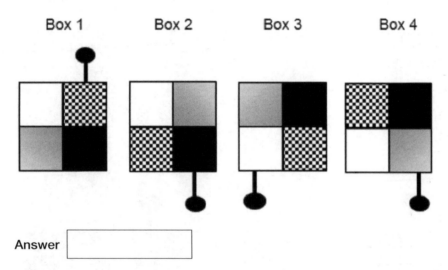

Answer

Question 2

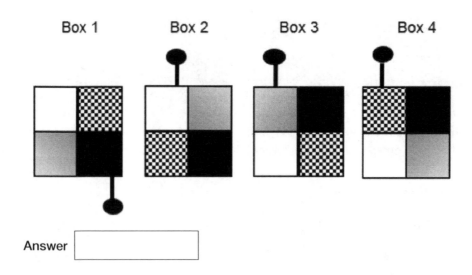

Answer [   ]

Question 3

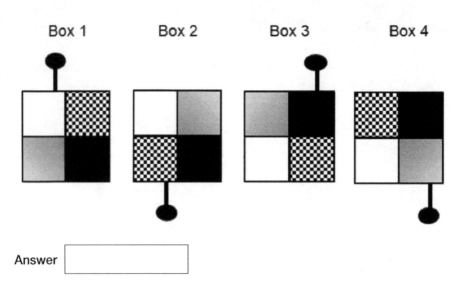

Answer [   ]

Question 4

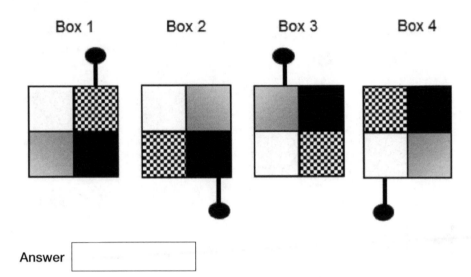

Answer [   ]

Question 5

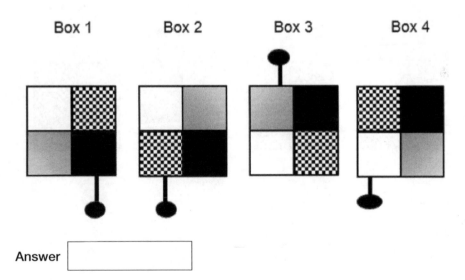

Answer [   ]

Question 6

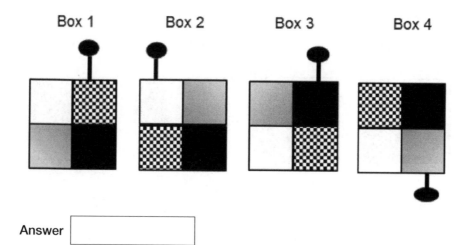

Answer _____

Question 7

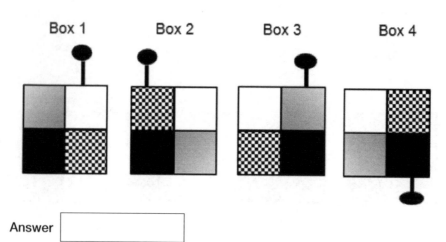

Answer _____

Question 8

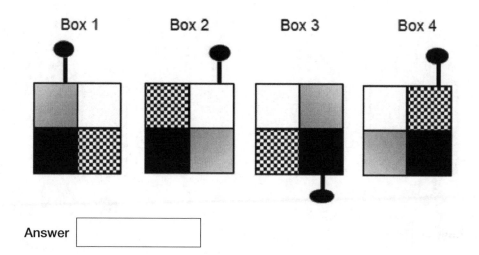

Answer

Question 9

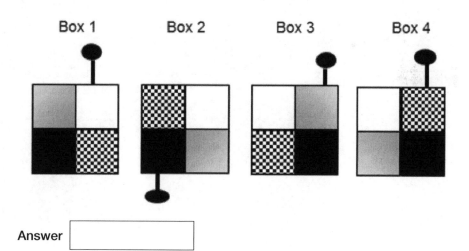

Answer

Question 10

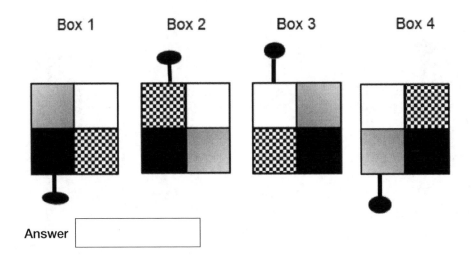

Answer

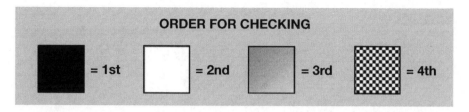

For the following ten questions, write down the order in which the boxes should be checked using the 'Order for Checking' sequence above:

Question 11

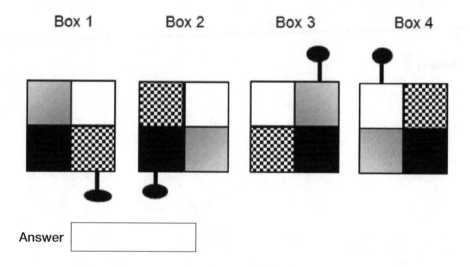

Answer [   ]

Question 12

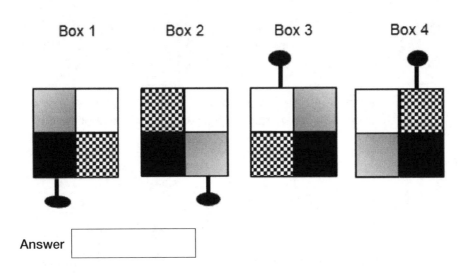

Answer

Question 13

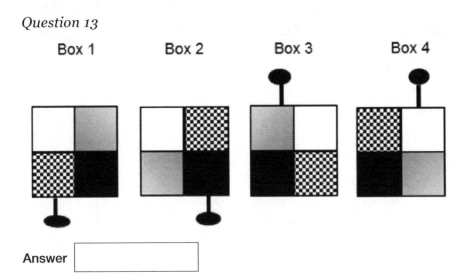

Answer

Question 14

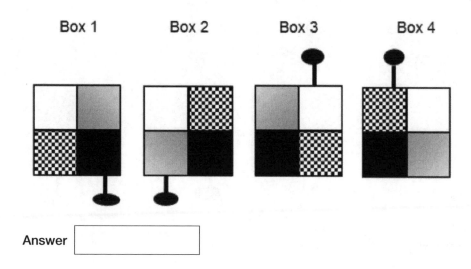

Answer

Question 15

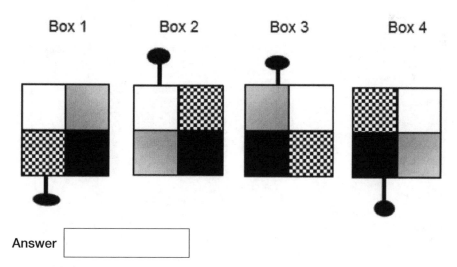

Answer

Question 16

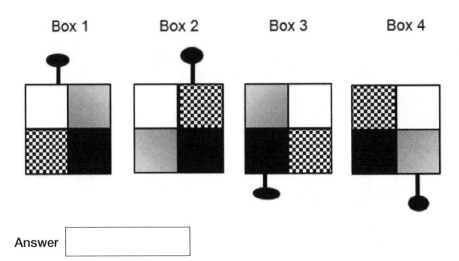

Answer [ ]

Question 17

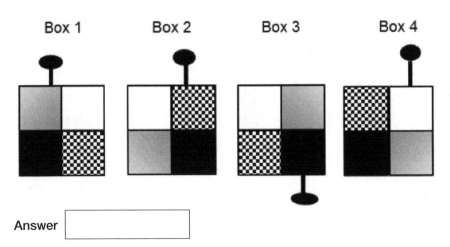

Answer [ ]

Question 18

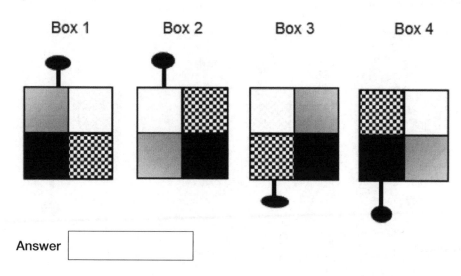

Answer [   ]

Question 19

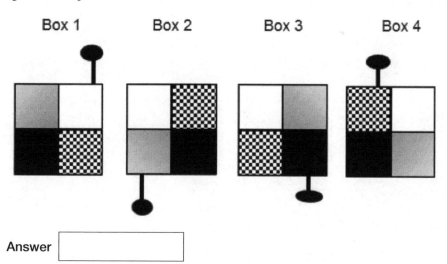

Answer [   ]

Question 20

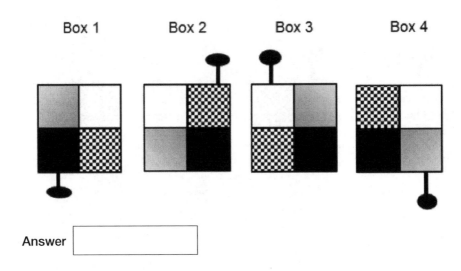

Box 1   Box 2   Box 3   Box 4

Answer

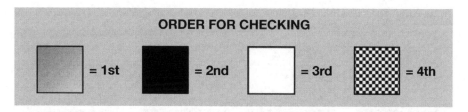

For the following five questions, write down the order in which the boxes should be checked using the 'Order for Checking' sequence above

Question 21

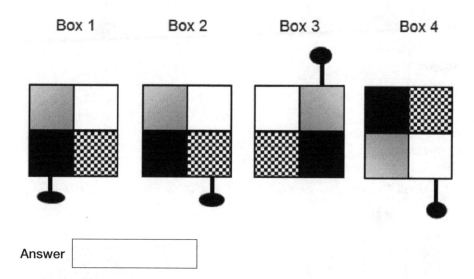

Answer

Question 22

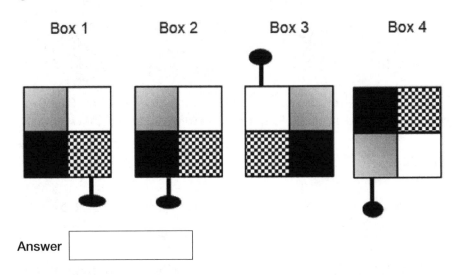

Answer [   ]

Question 23

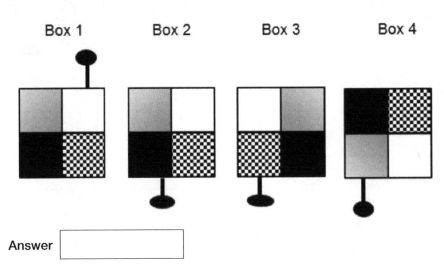

Answer [   ]

Question 24

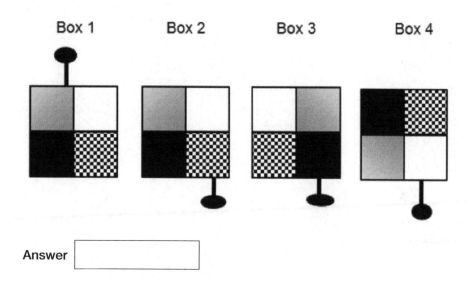

Answer [   ]

Question 25

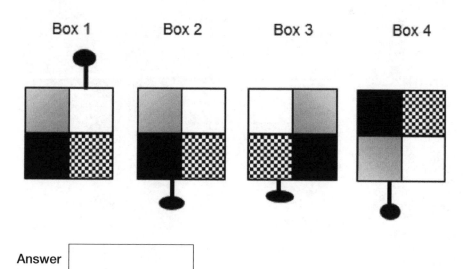

Answer [   ]

ANSWERS TO CHECKING TESTS - **TEST SECTION 2**

Q1.   3124

Q2.   2413

Q3.   1234

Q4.   4123

Q5.   4213

Q6.   2134

Q7.   1243

Q8.   2431

Q9.   1423

Q10. 3214

Q11. 2431

Q12. 1324

Q13. 2431

Q14. 1324

Q15. 4231

Q16. 3142

Q17. 3412

Q18. 4213

Q19. 3124

Q20. 1342

Q21. 3142

Q22. 4231

Q23. 4213

Q24. 1342

Q25. 4213

CHAPTER THREE
TRAIN DRIVER ERROR CHECKING TEST (TD-ECT)

During your Train Driver assessment, you will be expected to take a test that is designed to assess the key skills and qualities required by anyone who wishes to become a Train Driver. As an aspiring Train Driver, you will need to demonstrate high levels of skills in the following areas:

- Concentration
- Attention to detail
- Awareness
- Perseverance

The Train Driver Error Checking Test (TD-ECT) is a test primarily designed to assess these particular areas in order to improve your overall performance. Created by How2become, this Train Driver practice test allows you to practice and prepare for your assessment. ***Please note, that whilst we have provided practice questions, the Train Driver Error Checking Test (TD-ECT) is not an official Train Driving test.*** It is a test created by our team for you to gain a clearer understanding of the nature of the test, and the typical skills that are often evaluated.

ABOUT THE TRAIN DRIVER ERROR CHECKING TEST (TD-ECT)

The Train Driver Error Checking Test is an assessment that allows aspiring Train Drivers to practice their skills in order to prepare them for their assessment. The test measures particular skills, particularly focussing on concentration ability and attention to detail. These skills will be put to the test by measuring a person's ability to recognise errors in diagram formations.

Becoming a Train Driver requires a great deal of perseverance, and much of that perseverance comes from practicing. The more a person practices prior to their assessment, the more comfortable and confident they will feel in regards to their test. Thus, it is imperative that, whilst we cannot provide an exact account of what to expect in your actual test, we can provide questions that will focus on the necessary skills and qualities Train Drivers must possess in order to be successful during the selection process.

SAMPLE QUESTION

In order to answer the following questions, you must become familiar with the structure and format. You will need to apply rules and instructions to the questions in order to assess the error that is present.

During these practice questions, you will be given a set of diagrams for which you need to find the errors, using the Error Code Chart provided. The Error Code Chart are the codes that you will need to use to answer all of the questions.

The Error Code Chart will remain the same throughout the test, and is shown below:

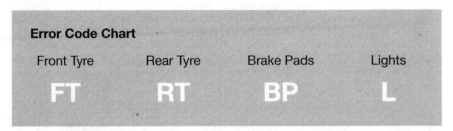

You will then be given 6 questions based on an Error Reference Chart. This will need to be used and remembered to determine which errors the bicycles have. The bicycles may have one or more errors. You will be able to work out the errors based on the reference codes and whether they are the same. If the bicycle does not have the same reference code, then there is an error.

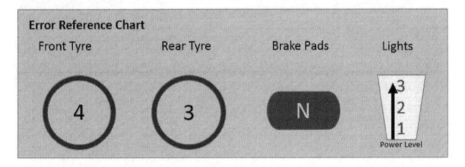

The Error Reference Chart is formulated above.

Using the Error Reference Chart, you must place the correct error code for each question. For Each Reference Chart, it will contain 6 questions. You will need to work out where the errors lie in the diagram.

Using the above Error Reference Chart, and using the Error Codes, find the error in the following diagram.

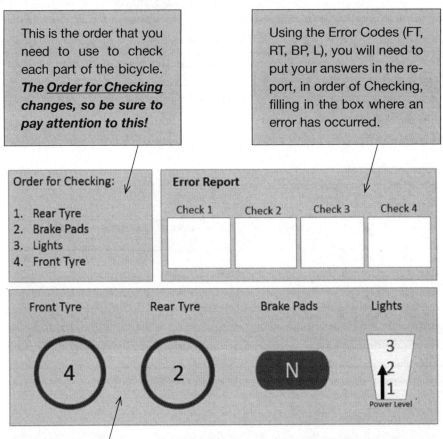

This is the order that you need to use to check each part of the bicycle. **The _Order for Checking_ changes, so be sure to pay attention to this!**

Using the Error Codes (FT, RT, BP, L), you will need to put your answers in the report, in order of Checking, filling in the box where an error has occurred.

Order for Checking:

1. Rear Tyre
2. Brake Pads
3. Lights
4. Front Tyre

Error Report

Check 1	Check 2	Check 3	Check 4

Front Tyre — 4

Rear Tyre — 2

Brake Pads — N

Lights — 3 2 1 Power Level

This set of diagrams need to be analysed carefully. You will have been given a Reference Chart to study before the question. Your task is to use that Reference Chart and cross-reference any errors in this set of diagrams. If a reference is different in the question, compared to that found on the Reference Chart, that means there is an error, and you would need to write it in the correct box in your report.

ANSWER FOR SAMPLE QUESTION:

Error Report			
Check 1	Check 2	Check 3	Check 4
RT	–	**L**	–

- For Check 1, using the order for checking, you need to check the Rear Tyre. Using the Reference Chart, the Rear Tyre is referenced '3', whereas in the question it is referenced '2'. This shows an error, because the references do not match. Therefore, you would need to write RT in the Check 1 box.

- For Check 2, using the order for checking, you would need to check the Brake Pads. Using the Reference Chart, the Brake Pads are referenced 'N'; in the question, the Brake Pads are also referenced 'N', therefore shows no error. In order to mark no error in the box', simply put a line through the box.

- For Check 3, using the order for checking, you would need to check the Lights. Using the Reference Chart, the Lights are referenced with the power '1-3'; in the question the Lights are only powered to '2'. This shows an error, because the references do not match. Therefore, you would to write L in the Check 3 box.

- For Check 4, using the order for checking, you would need to check the Front Tyre. Using the Reference Chart, the Front Tyre is referenced '4;' in the question, the Front Tyre is also referenced '4'. This shows no error, and you should draw a line through the box, indicating that there is no error.

Using the above system, work through the questions as quickly and as effectively as you can. Remember, the point of these types of questions is to measure speed, as well as accuracy.

Make sure that you read all the information on the Reference Chart, before attempting to answer the six questions that relate. For each question, it is vitally important that you check what order you need to assess first. You will lose easy marks for lack of attention to detail.

TD-ECT, SECTION 1

Error Code Chart

Front Tyre	Rear Tyre	Brake Pads	Lights
FT	**RT**	**BP**	**L**

The above Chart is a reminder of the Error Codes that you will need to insert into the Error Report for each error you find.

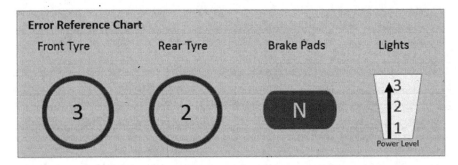

Error Reference Chart

Front Tyre	Rear Tyre	Brake Pads	Lights

Using the Error Reference Chart above, *answer questions 1 to 6,* based on the information found in this chart.

For the **next 6 questions**, use the above Error Reference Chart to determine which errors the bicycle have. If the bicycle does not have the same reference, then there is an error.

Only enter a code if there is an error present! If an error is not present, draw a line through the box.

Question 1.

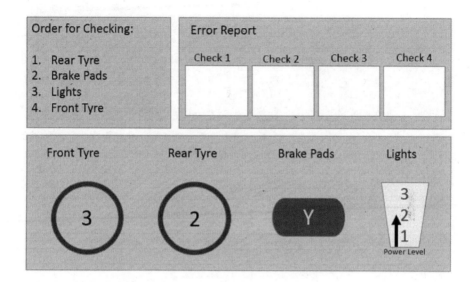

Order for Checking:

1. Rear Tyre
2. Brake Pads
3. Lights
4. Front Tyre

Error Report

Check 1	Check 2	Check 3	Check 4

Front Tyre — 3
Rear Tyre — 2
Brake Pads — Y
Lights — Power Level 3 2 1

Question 2.

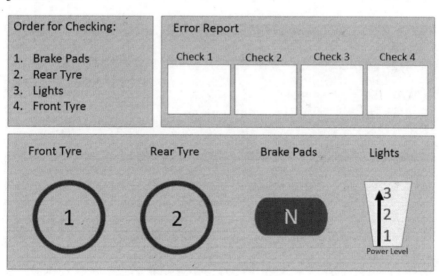

Order for Checking:

1. Brake Pads
2. Rear Tyre
3. Lights
4. Front Tyre

Error Report

Check 1	Check 2	Check 3	Check 4

Front Tyre — 1
Rear Tyre — 2
Brake Pads — N
Lights — Power Level 3 2 1

Question 3.

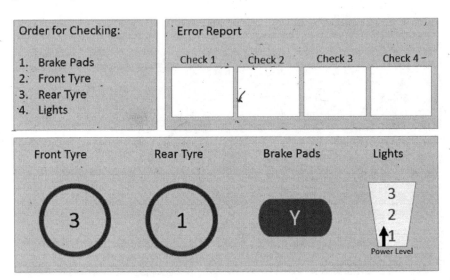

Question 4.

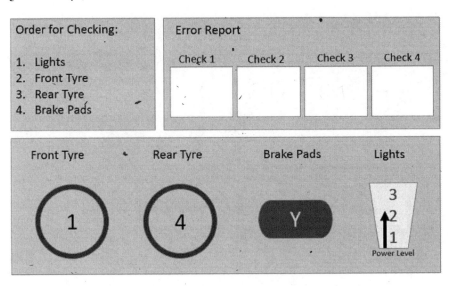

Question 5.

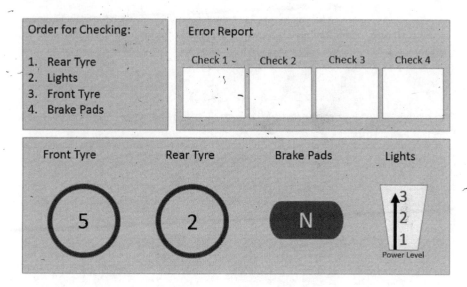

Order for Checking:

1. Rear Tyre
2. Lights
3. Front Tyre
4. Brake Pads

Error Report

Check 1	Check 2	Check 3	Check 4

Front Tyre: 5
Rear Tyre: 2
Brake Pads: N
Lights: Power Level (3, 2, 1)

Question 6.

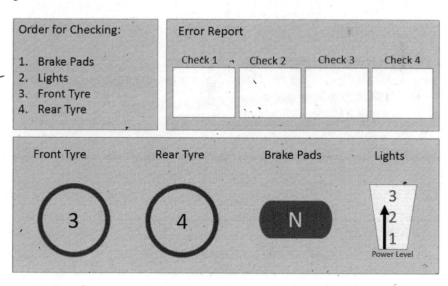

Order for Checking:

1. Brake Pads
2. Lights
3. Front Tyre
4. Rear Tyre

Error Report

Check 1	Check 2	Check 3	Check 4

Front Tyre: 3
Rear Tyre: 4
Brake Pads: N
Lights: Power Level (3, 2, 1)

Error Code Chart

Front Tyre	Rear Tyre	Brake Pads	Lights
FT	RT	BP	L

The above Chart is a reminder of the Error Codes that you will need to insert into the Error Report for each error you find.

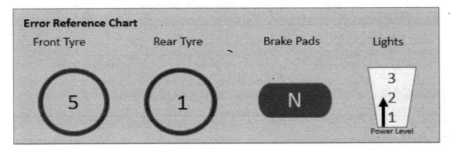

Error Reference Chart

Front Tyre	Rear Tyre	Brake Pads	Lights
5	1	N	3 2 1 Power Level

Using the Error Reference Chart above, *answer questions 7 to 12*, based on the information found in this chart.

For the **next 6 questions**, use the above Error Reference Chart to determine which errors the bicycle have. If the bicycle does not have the same reference, then there is an error.

Only enter a code if there is an error present! If an error is not present, draw a line through the box.

Question 7.

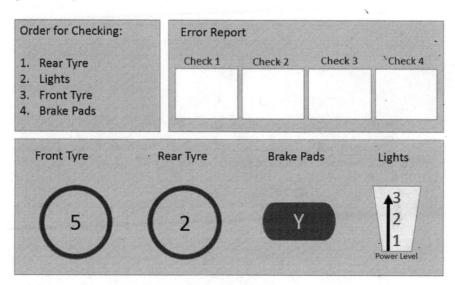

Question 8.

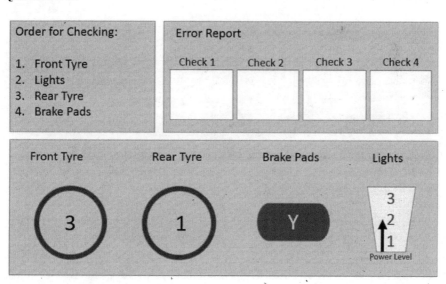

Question 9.

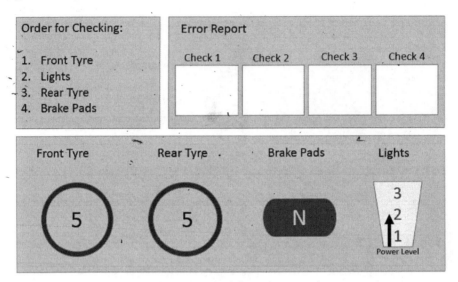

Order for Checking:

1. Front Tyre
2. Lights
3. Rear Tyre
4. Brake Pads

Error Report

Check 1	Check 2	Check 3	Check 4

Front Tyre — 5
Rear Tyre — 5
Brake Pads — N
Lights — 3 2 1 Power Level

Question 10.

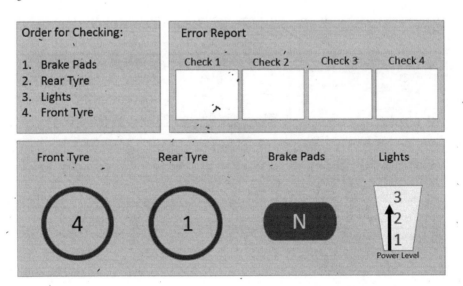

Order for Checking:

1. Brake Pads
2. Rear Tyre
3. Lights
4. Front Tyre

Error Report

Check 1	Check 2	Check 3	Check 4

Front Tyre — 4
Rear Tyre — 1
Brake Pads — N
Lights — 3 2 1 Power Level

Question 11.

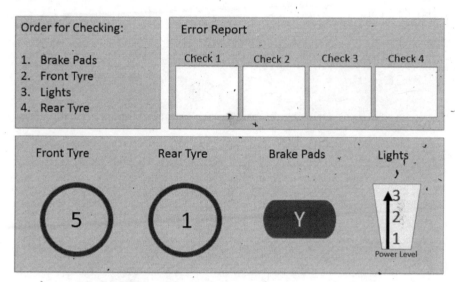

Order for Checking:

1. Brake Pads
2. Front Tyre
3. Lights
4. Rear Tyre

Error Report

Check 1   Check 2   Check 3   Check 4

Front Tyre   Rear Tyre   Brake Pads   Lights

5   1   Y   Power Level

Question 12.

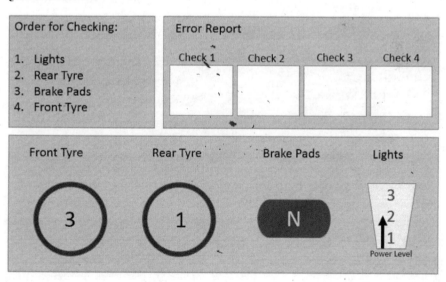

Order for Checking:

1. Lights
2. Rear Tyre
3. Brake Pads
4. Front Tyre

Error Report

Check 1   Check 2   Check 3   Check 4

Front Tyre   Rear Tyre   Brake Pads   Lights

3   1   N   Power Level

ANSWERS TO TRAIN DRIVER ERROR CHECKING TEST – (SECTION 1)

Question 1.

Error Report			
Check 1	Check 2	Check 3	Check 4
–	**BP**	**L**	–

Question 2.

Error Report			
Check 1	Check 2	Check 3	Check 4
–	–	–	**FT**

Question 3.

Error Report			
Check 1	Check 2	Check 3	Check 4
BP	–	**RT**	**L**

Question 4.

Error Report			
Check 1	Check 2	Check 3	Check 4
L	**FT**	**RT**	**BP**

Question 5.

Error Report			
Check 1	Check 2	Check 3	Check 4
—	—	**FT**	—

Question 6.

Error Report			
Check 1	Check 2	Check 3	Check 4
—	**L**	—	**RT**

Question 7.

Error Report			
Check 1	Check 2	Check 3	Check 4
RT	**L**	—	**BP**

Question 8.

Error Report			
Check 1	Check 2	Check 3	Check 4
FT	—	—	**BP**

Question 9.

Error Report			
Check 1	Check 2	Check 3	Check 4
–	–	**RT**	–

Question 10.

Error Report			
Check 1	Check 2	Check 3	Check 4
–	–	**L**	**FT**

Question 11.

Error Report			
Check 1	Check 2	Check 3	Check 4
BP	–	**L**	–

Question 12.

Error Report			
Check 1	Check 2	Check 3	Check 4
–	–	–	**FT**

TD-ECT, SECTION 2

Error Code Chart

Front Tyre	Rear Tyre	Brake Pads	Lights
FT	**RT**	**BP**	**L**

The above Chart is a reminder of the Error Codes that you will need to insert into the Error Report for each error you find.

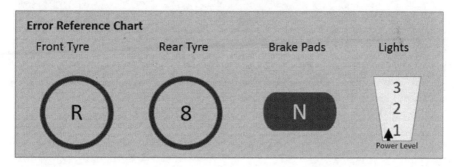

The above Chart is a reminder of the Error Codes that you will need to insert into the Error Report for each error you find.

Using the Error Reference Chart above, *answer questions 1 to 6*, based on the information found in this chart.

For the **next 6 questions**, use the above Error Reference Chart to determine which errors the bicycle have. If the bicycle does not have the same reference, then there is an error.

Only enter a code if there is an error present! If an error is not present, draw a line through the box.

Question 1.

Order for Checking:	Error Report			
	Check 1	Check 2	Check 3	Check 4
1. Lights				
2. Rear Tyre				
3. Brake Pads				
4. Front Tyre				

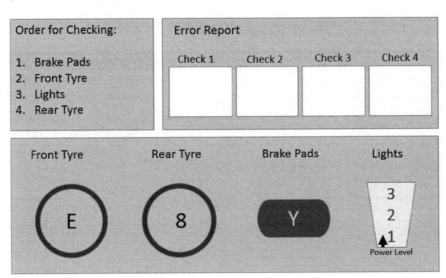

Question 2.

Order for Checking:	Error Report			
	Check 1	Check 2	Check 3	Check 4
1. Brake Pads				
2. Front Tyre				
3. Lights				
4. Rear Tyre				

Question 3.

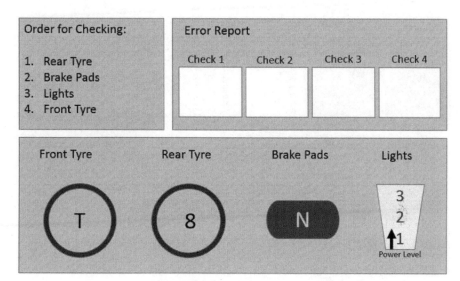

Question 4.

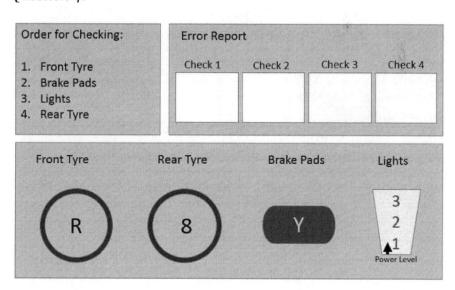

Question 5.

Order for Checking:

1. Lights
2. Brake Pads
3. Rear Tyre
4. Front Tyre

Error Report

Check 1	Check 2	Check 3	Check 4

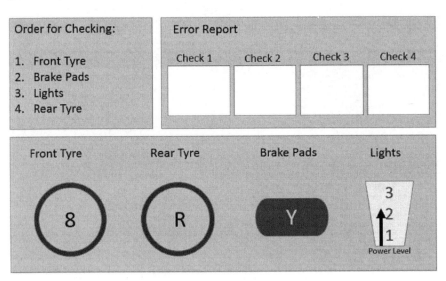

Question 6.

Order for Checking:

1. Front Tyre
2. Brake Pads
3. Lights
4. Rear Tyre

Error Report

Check 1	Check 2	Check 3	Check 4

Error Code Chart

Front Tyre	Rear Tyre	Brake Pads	Lights
FT	**RT**	**BP**	**L**

The above Chart is a reminder of the Error Codes that you will need to insert into the Error Report for each error you find.

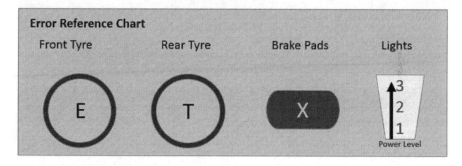

Using the Error Reference Chart above, *answer questions 7 to 12*, based on the information found in this chart.

For the **next 6 questions**, use the above Error Reference Chart to determine which errors the bicycle have. If the bicycle does not have the same reference, then there is an error.

Only enter a code if there is an error present! If an error is not present, draw a line through the box.

Question 7.

Order for Checking:	Error Report			
1. Lights	Check 1	Check 2	Check 3	Check 4
2. Brake Pads				
3. Rear Tyre				
4. Front Tyre				

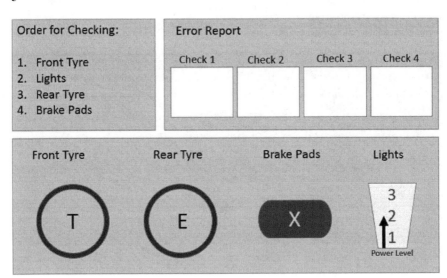

Question 8.

Order for Checking:	Error Report			
1. Front Tyre	Check 1	Check 2	Check 3	Check 4
2. Lights				
3. Rear Tyre				
4. Brake Pads				

Question 9.

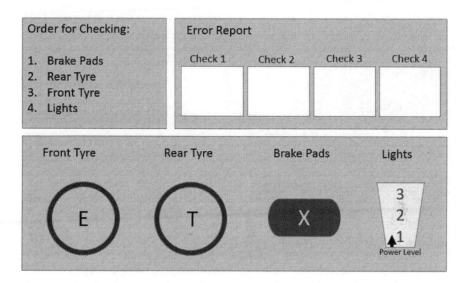

Question 10.

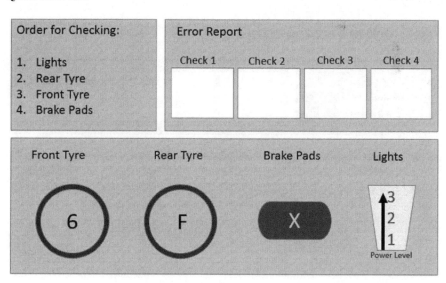

Question 11.

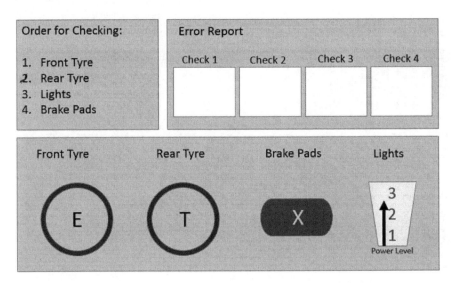

Order for Checking:	Error Report			
	Check 1	Check 2	Check 3	Check 4
1. Lights				
2. Rear Tyre				
3. Front Tyre				
4. Brake Pads				

Front Tyre	Rear Tyre	Brake Pads	Lights
E	I	N	3 2 1 Power Level

Question 12.

Order for Checking:	Error Report			
	Check 1	Check 2	Check 3	Check 4
1. Front Tyre				
2. Rear Tyre				
3. Lights				
4. Brake Pads				

Front Tyre	Rear Tyre	Brake Pads	Lights
E	T	X	3 2 1 Power Level

ANSWERS TO TRAIN DRIVER ERROR CHECKING TEST (SECTION 2)

Question 1.

Error Report			
Check 1	Check 2	Check 3	Check 4
L	RT	BP	–

Question 2.

Error Report			
Check 1	Check 2	Check 3	Check 4
BP	FT	–	–

Question 3.

Error Report			
Check 1	Check 2	Check 3	Check 4
–	–	L	FT

Question 4.

Error Report			
Check 1	Check 2	Check 3	Check 4
–	BP	–	–

Question 5.

Error Report			
Check 1	Check 2	Check 3	Check 4
L	–	RT	–

Question 6.

Error Report			
Check 1	Check 2	Check 3	Check 4
FT	BP	L	RT

Question 7.

Error Report			
Check 1	Check 2	Check 3	Check 4
–	BP	RT	FT

Question 8.

Error Report			
Check 1	Check 2	Check 3	Check 4
FT	L	RT	–

Question 9.

Error Report			
Check 1	Check 2	Check 3	Check 4
–	–	–	L

Question 10.

Error Report			
Check 1	Check 2	Check 3	Check 4
–	RT	FT	–

Question 11.

Error Report			
Check 1	Check 2	Check 3	Check 4
–	RT	–	BP

Question 12.

Error Report			
Check 1	Check 2	Check 3	Check 4
–	–	L	–

CHAPTER FOUR
NUMERICAL CONCENTRATION TESTS

Numerical Comparison Tests are a form of assessment which are designed to measure a candidate's ability and proficiency at comparing combinations of digits, and determine which combination of digits is not the same.

The test itself can be assessed in two ways. Firstly, some companies use a numerical comparison test which uses sets of numbers, and you have to find the digits that do not match. Whereas other tests can focus on alpha-numerical digits which comprise of letters and numbers. Both types of tests assess the same thing in terms of concentration and time keeping skills.

Numerical Comparison tests are a great psychometric test that can help you prepare for your Train Driver Tests. Whilst this test will not form part of your Train Driver assessment, we believe it is a great way to improve your concentration skills; a key skill for Train Drivers.

For this test, we will provide you with two sample tests, each containing 150 questions, which you should aim to complete in 5 minutes. Now, you may be thinking that this is a lot of questions to answer in a small time frame, but the idea of these types of tests is so you are unable to finish them. It is better to answer 50 questions and get them all right, as opposed to answering 80 questions and getting 30 wrong.

Look at the four pairs of numerical digits. Circle or highlight the combination pair that **does not** match.

Sheet 1

7956	9756	7952	7952	7944	7944	7950	7950
4654	4654	6997	6997	2629	2669	2697	2697
6594	6594	9892	9882	8502	8502	7982	7982
9872	9872	2600	2600	5987	5987	2698	2689

7952	7952	7952	7952	9562	9526	4953	4953
2657	2657	2326	2326	2654	2654	2659	2659
8798	8798	4694	4649	4622	4622	8987	8887
2620	2260	4698	4698	2367	2367	7952	7952

5952	5952	5947	5947	9795	9795	6529	6592
2626	2266	4955	4955	2658	6258	7985	7985
4987	4987	5698	5698	0544	0544	1658	1658
7952	7952	8954	8945	9897	9897	1469	1469

4956	4956	8987	8987	7951	7951	9456	4956
4597	4597	5256	5526	1698	1698	5977	5977
7952	7925	4620	4620	8971	8971	7995	7995
2669	2669	2698	2698	1127	1172	2659	2659

4956	4956	4697	4697	1036	1036	0641	6041
2697	2697	9795	9985	5897	5897	1617	1617
7951	7951	2698	2698	0464	0446	7952	7952
0367	0376	7951	7951	2657	2657	0659	0659

4972	4972	7102	7102	7946	9746	7952	7952
2679	2679	2687	2687	1649	1649	2647	2647
5978	5987	4952	4922	7951	7951	7953	7593
9891	9891	0625	0625	2648	2648	0264	0264

5954	5954	4725	4725	7915	7951	4912	4912
2697	2679	0659	0659	3698	3698	2987	2987
3679	3679	8974	9874	7984	7984	7985	7985
3255	3255	1659	1659	1657	1657	2659	2695

Look at the four pairs of numerical digits. Circle or highlight the combination pair that **does not** match.

Sheet 2

26221 26221	49589 49879	49897 49897	49587 49587
45987 54987	49788 49788	58952 58952	79526 79526
79526 79526	59598 59598	29598 92598	26297 26927
26987 26987	89532 89532	79852 79852	79581 79581
69578 69578	79595 79595	49846 49846	78952 88952
89526 89526	89874 89874	65987 65987	06297 06297
65697 65697	46922 46922	49287 49278	79852 79852
98955 89955	59877 59787	95120 95120	06579 06579
49526 49526	79526 79526	49562 49562	79562 79562
67942 67942	26779 26779	26597 26579	26589 26589
36957 36957	65105 65150	79582 79582	79526 79526
79520 79502	49785 49785	25957 25957	26997 26979
79529 79592	59563 59563	79885 79885	49795 49795
59872 59872	78966 78966	26972 26972	26984 26984
26979 26979	78925 78965	26997 62997	49520 49520
95878 95878	39875 39875	62065 62065	29578 29587
45952 45952	74628 74628	49795 49795	49587 94587
98794 98794	59532 55932	26304 26304	59852 59852
36489 36489	26487 26487	79852 79852	23264 23264
66448 64648	79561 79561	26297 26279	49875 49875
98952 98952	49526 49526	79582 79582	49878 49878
26984 26994	26597 26597	26978 26978	69795 69795
49562 49562	79810 78910	79556 79566	59871 59871
19894 19894	06094 06094	56594 56594	06578 60578
59526 55926	45978 45978	79321 79321	14995 14995
62548 62548	26544 26454	23940 23904	89814 89814
02645 02645	79453 79453	26048 26048	19632 19632
10594 10594	13258 13258	06585 06585	26959 26599

Look at the four pairs of numerical digits. Circle or highlight the combination pair that **does not** match.

Sheet 3

59547	59547	49898	49898	59547	59547	49562	49652
59594	59994	59521	59521	36985	36985	23626	23626
49987	49987	49636	94636	26245	22245	49879	49879
79820	79820	49875	49875	50267	50267	46210	46210

6259	6259	4985	4985	4957	4957	47952	47952
5959	5959	2954	2945	9562	9562	26294	26924
7985	9785	4987	4987	2627	2672	79582	79582
2625	2625	1020	1020	7981	7981	26297	26297

49594	94594	49595	49595	45695	45695	56595	56595
49872	49872	29877	29877	59887	59887	55977	55797
26987	26987	78945	78945	79562	79562	78451	78451
79562	79562	18787	18887	26987	29687	18598	18598

4620	4620	7952	7952	79522	79252	45695	45695
2695	6295	2695	2695	26878	26878	59741	59741
3975	3975	7762	7726	78762	78762	05144	05144
3971	3971	0136	0136	26649	26649	48740	47840

45695	45695	79856	79856	46547	46547	94695	94695
45788	45878	26971	26971	26298	26289	26541	26541
98522	98522	16026	16206	89523	89523	01259	10259
02154	02154	56987	56987	32647	32647	79525	79525

47987	47789	49562	49562	47952	47952	79526	79526
46259	46259	26967	62967	26958	26958	56978	56798
89856	89856	79565	79565	89871	89871	79812	79812
26587	26587	56597	56597	16598	61598	16164	16164

4953	4953	4957	4957	7954	7994	46956	46956
6106	6106	7956	7965	1959	1959	26526	26526
5998	5989	6298	6298	9515	9515	46956	46596
4695	4695	7951	7951	6956	6956	16625	16625

Look at the four pairs of numerical digits. Circle or highlight the combination pair that **does not** match.

Sheet 4

495962 495962	792506 792506	134657 134657	165498 165498
265548 265548	648621 648621	579156 579516	898632 898632
499856 498956	985614 895614	461227 461227	265479 264579
565654 565654	465975 465975	756798 756798	795612 795612

987659 987569	469579 469579	495631 495631	469562 469562
974064 974064	943146 493146	146476 146476	656545 656545
364896 364896	346439 346439	659782 659782	963272 936272
647820 647820	124057 124057	332016 332061	120368 120368

465653 465563	695653 695653	495652 495652	495762 495762
327985 327985	369745 369745	232264 322264	968421 968421
361410 361410	456958 456958	469789 469789	023058 020358
979862 979862	565410 565401	203246 203246	875653 875653

496562 496562	989523 989532	465620 465620	479562 749562
658978 658987	659874 659874	236988 326988	356445 356445
746982 746982	456025 456025	898741 898741	289851 289851
456984 456984	620462 620462	136265 136265	629878 629878

462300 462300	795843 795843	794623 794623	795623 795623
656875 656875	367462 364762	465795 465795	462321 462321
794613 794613	128954 128954	986561 986561	120657 126057
135896 315896	367589 367589	213015 123015	036980 036980

479562 475962	469253 469253	795623 795623	795320 795320
845841 845841	232644 232644	469741 469741	256958 256958
463286 463286	031659 301659	283917 283197	476232 476223
236367 236367	123568 123568	461973 461973	794628 794628

956231 956213	496532 496532	469230 469230	479623 479623
632326 632326	236597 236597	326597 326597	265644 265644
795620 795620	444598 444598	795621 759621	623055 623505
065958 065958	632554 632254	165844 165844	112025 112025

Look at the four pairs of numerical digits. Circle or highlight the combination pair that **does not** match.

Sheet 5

45478 45478	48952 48925	16645 16645	49526 49526
79865 79865	29548 29548	26594 26954	45695 45695
62610 62610	48145 48145	49897 49897	26548 26458
48879 84879	48778 48778	84514 84514	59540 59540
59564 59564	79562 79562	49589 49589	49579 49579
49878 49878	26589 26598	78992 87992	95214 95214
79556 79555	79514 79514	29018 29018	46498 46498
56201 56201	14698 14698	48405 48405	95212 95221
14957 14957	49597 49597	49784 49784	79526 79526
89566 89565	59059 59059	29852 29852	29578 29578
56424 56424	01462 01462	26014 26041	47841 47841
98970 98970	02649 20649	49878 49878	15887 15587
49562 94562	44926 44926	49875 49875	90895 90895
26579 26579	65897 65987	69874 69874	59005 59005
89825 89825	79852 79852	16984 61984	98994 98994
26215 26215	26597 26597	49802 49802	94875 94847
79569 79569	79556 75956	46562 46562	49562 49562
59878 59878	56978 56978	65987 65897	00326 00326
57841 57814	79562 79562	79523 79523	46645 64645
16959 16959	26597 26597	26547 26547	79561 79561
47956 47596	49622 49622	46224 46224	49562 49562
26598 26598	29974 29974	49856 49865	26987 26897
79841 79841	49856 49856	59878 59878	79564 79564
13021 13021	29578 92578	62348 62348	46232 46232
14626 14626	74796 77496	46952 46952	49797 49797
59875 95875	26994 26994	79855 79585	46956 46956
49516 49516	79565 79565	79562 79562	26982 26982
62597 62597	56597 56597	26979 26979	26214 26124

Look at the four pairs of numerical digits. Circle or highlight the combination pair that **does not** match.

Sheet 6

79562 97562	47956 47596	49656 49656	49768 49768
25958 25958	26589 26589	26989 26989	86598 86598
79856 79856	79856 79856	79562 79562	89564 98564
56244 56244	59578 59578	62987 26987	46298 46298
79556 79556	41962 41962	79564 97564	16266 16266
59597 59579	29877 29787	46629 46629	46525 46525
79656 79656	79562 79562	97956 97956	89561 89561
59897 59897	26598 26598	56249 56249	46458 46548
49526 49526	49876 49786		
59879 59879	56597 56597		
78949 78949	79561 79561		
97896 97869	16197 16197		

ANSWERS TO TEST 1

Sheet 1

7956	9756	7952	7952	7944	7944	7950	7950
4654	4654	6997	6997	2629	2669	2697	2697
6594	6594	9892	9882	8502	8502	7982	7982
9872	9872	2600	2600	5987	5987	2698	2689
7952	7952	7952	7952	9562	9526	4953	4953
2657	2657	2326	2326	2654	2654	2659	2659
8798	8798	4694	4649	4622	4622	8987	8887
2620	2260	4698	4698	2367	2367	7952	7952
5952	5952	5947	5947	9795	9795	6529	6592
2626	2266	4955	4955	2658	6258	7985	7985
4987	4987	5698	5698	0544	0544	1658	1658
7952	7952	8954	8945	9897	9897	1469	1469
4956	4956	8987	8987	7951	7951	9456	4956
4597	4597	5256	5526	1698	1698	5977	5977
7952	7925	4620	4620	8971	8971	7995	7995
2669	2669	2698	2698	1127	1172	2659	2659
4956	4956	4697	4697	1036	1036	0641	6041
2697	2697	9795	9985	5897	5897	1617	1617
7951	7951	2698	2698	0464	0446	7952	7952
0367	0376	7951	7951	2657	2657	0659	0659
4972	4972	7102	7102	7946	9746	7952	7952
2679	2679	2687	2687	1649	1649	2647	2647
5978	5987	4952	4922	7951	7951	7953	7593
9891	9891	0625	0625	2648	2648	0264	0264
5954	5954	4725	4725	7915	7951	4912	4912
2697	2679	0659	0659	3698	3698	2987	2987
3679	3679	8974	9874	7984	7984	7985	7985
3255	3255	1659	1659	1657	1657	2659	2695

Sheet 2

26221 26221	49589 49879	49897 49897	49587 49587
45987 54987	49788 49788	58952 58952	79526 79526
79526 79526	59598 59598	29598 92598	26297 26927
26987 26987	89532 89532	79852 79852	79581 79581
69578 69578	79595 79595	49846 49846	78952 88952
89526 89526	89874 89874	65987 65987	06297 06297
65697 65697	46922 46922	49287 49278	79852 79852
98955 89955	59877 59787	95120 95120	06579 06579
49526 49526	79526 79526	49562 49562	79562 79562
67942 67942	26779 26779	26597 26579	26589 26589
36957 36957	65105 65150	79582 79582	79526 79526
79520 79502	49785 49785	25957 25957	26997 26979
79529 79592	59563 59563	79885 79885	49795 49795
59872 59872	78966 78966	26972 26972	26984 26984
26979 26979	78925 78965	26997 62997	49520 49520
95878 95878	39875 39875	62065 62065	29578 29587
45952 45952	74628 74628	49795 49795	49587 94587
98794 98794	59532 55932	26304 26304	59852 59852
36489 36489	26487 26487	79852 79852	23264 23264
66448 64648	79561 79561	26297 26279	49875 49875
98952 98952	49526 49526	79582 79582	49878 49878
26984 26994	26597 26597	26978 26978	69795 69795
49562 49562	79810 78910	79556 79566	59871 59871
19894 19894	06094 06094	56594 56594	06578 60578
59526 55926	45978 45978	79321 79321	14995 14995
62548 62548	26544 26454	23940 23904	89814 89814
02645 02645	79453 79453	26048 26048	19632 19632
10594 10594	13258 13258	06585 06585	26959 26599

Sheet 3

59547 59547	49898 49898	59547 59547	49562 49652
59594 59994	59521 59521	36985 36985	23626 23626
49987 49987	49636 94636	26245 22245	49879 49879
79820 79820	49875 49875	50267 50267	46210 46210

6259 6259	4985 4985	4957 4957	47952 47952
5959 5959	2954 2945	9562 9562	26294 26924
7985 9785	4987 4987	2627 2672	79582 79582
2625 2625	1020 1020	7981 7981	26297 26297

49594 94594	49595 49595	45695 45695	56595 56595
49872 49872	29877 29877	59887 59887	55977 55797
26987 26987	78945 78945	79562 79562	78451 78451
79562 79562	18787 18887	26987 29687	18598 18598

4620 4620	7952 7952	79522 79252	45695 45695
2695 6295	2695 2695	26878 26878	59741 59741
3975 3975	7762 7726	78762 78762	05144 05144
3971 3971	0136 0136	26649 26649	48740 47840

45695 45695	79856 79856	46547 46547	94695 94695
45788 45878	26971 26971	26298 26289	26541 26541
98522 98522	16026 16206	89523 89523	01259 10259
02154 02154	56987 56987	32647 32647	79525 79525

47987 47789	49562 49562	47952 47952	79526 79526
46259 46259	26967 62967	26958 26958	56978 56798
89856 89856	79565 79565	89871 89871	79812 79812
26587 26587	56597 56597	16598 61598	16164 16164

4953 4953	4957 4957	7954 7994	46956 46956
6106 6106	7956 7965	1959 1959	26526 26526
5998 5989	6298 6298	9515 9515	46956 46596
4695 4695	7951 7951	6956 6956	16625 16625

Sheet 4

495962 495962	792506 792506	134657 134657	165498 165498
265548 265548	648621 648621	579156 579516	898632 898632
499856 498956	985614 895614	461227 461227	265479 264579
565654 565654	465975 465975	756798 756798	795612 795612
987659 987569	469579 469579	495631 495631	469562 469562
974064 974064	943146 493146	146476 146476	656545 656545
364896 364896	346439 346439	659782 659782	963272 936272
647820 647820	124057 124057	332016 332061	120368 120368
465653 465563	695653 695653	495652 495652	495762 495762
327985 327985	369745 369745	232264 322264	968421 968421
361410 361410	456958 456958	469789 469789	023058 020358
979862 979862	565410 565401	203246 203246	875653 875653
496562 496562	989523 989532	465620 465620	479562 749562
658978 658987	659874 659874	236988 326988	356445 356445
746982 746982	456025 456025	898741 898741	289851 289851
456984 456984	620462 620462	136265 136265	629878 629878
462300 462300	795843 795843	794623 794623	795623 795623
656875 656875	367462 364762	465795 465795	462321 462321
794613 794613	128954 128954	986561 986561	120657 126057
135896 315896	367589 367589	213015 123015	036980 036980
479562 475962	469253 469253	795623 795623	795320 795320
845841 845841	232644 232644	469741 469741	256958 256958
463286 463286	031659 301659	283917 283197	476232 476223
236367 236367	123568 123568	461973 461973	794628 794628
956231 956213	496532 496532	469230 469230	479623 479623
632326 632326	236597 236597	326597 326597	265644 265644
795620 795620	444598 444598	795621 759621	623055 623505
065958 065958	632554 632254	165844 165844	112025 112025

Sheet 5

45478 45478	48952 48925	16645 16645	49526 49526
79865 79865	29548 29548	26594 26954	45695 45695
62610 62610	48145 48145	49897 49897	26548 26458
48879 84879	48778 48778	84514 84514	59540 59540
59564 59564	79562 79562	49589 49589	49579 49579
49878 49878	26589 26598	78992 87992	95214 95214
79556 79555	79514 79514	29018 29018	46498 46498
56201 56201	14698 14698	48405 48405	95212 95221
14957 14957	49597 49597	49784 49784	79526 79526
89566 89565	59059 59059	29852 29852	29578 29578
56424 56424	01462 01462	26014 26041	47841 47841
98970 98970	02649 20649	49878 49878	15887 15587
49562 94562	44926 44926	49875 49875	90895 90895
26579 26579	65897 65987	69874 69874	59005 59005
89825 89825	79852 79852	16984 61984	98994 98994
26215 26215	26597 26597	49802 49802	94875 94847
79569 79569	79556 75956	46562 46562	49562 49562
59878 59878	56978 56978	65987 65897	00326 00326
57841 57814	79562 79562	79523 79523	46645 64645
16959 16959	26597 26597	26547 26547	79561 79561
47956 47596	49622 49622	46224 46224	49562 49562
26598 26598	29974 29974	49856 49865	26987 26897
79841 79841	49856 49856	59878 59878	79564 79564
13021 13021	29578 92578	62348 62348	46232 46232
14626 14626	74796 77496	46952 46952	49797 49797
59875 95875	26994 26994	79855 79585	46956 46956
49516 49516	79565 79565	79562 79562	26982 26982
62597 62597	56597 56597	26979 26979	26214 26124

Sheet 6

79562 97562	47956 47596	49656 49656	49768 49768
25958 25958	26589 26589	26989 26989	86598 86598
79856 79856	79856 79856	79562 79562	89564 98564
56244 56244	59578 59578	62987 26987	46298 46298
79556 79556	41962 41962	79564 97564	16266 16266
59597 59579	29877 29787	46629 46629	46525 46525
79656 79656	79562 79562	97956 97956	89561 89561
59897 59897	26598 26598	56249 56249	46458 46548
49526 49526	49876 49786		
59879 59879	56597 56597		
78949 78949	79561 79561		
97896 97869	16197 16197		

Look at the four pairs of numerical digits. Circle or highlight the combination pair that **does not** match.

Sheet 1

j07r	j07r	mv39	mv93	g39j	g39j	p20s	p20s
I086	i086	ru28	ru28	e2k0	e2k0	w95r	w95r
3e5d	3e5d	otr4	otr4	30ri	30ir	ccv4	cav4
u90f	u90f	03w2	03w2	e22f	e22f	fj3a	fj3a
qp20	pq20	hg94	hg94	34r9	34r9	ioa8	ioa8
cme3	cme3	lldk	lldk	e03i	e03i	yo65	yo65
eo03	eo03	30dp	3odp	f3k0	f3k0	v49f	u49f
r30i	r30i	wp20	wp20	mn03	nn03	g349	g349
fl02	fl02	daj5	daj5	fal4	fal4	3r0f	r30f
m98a	m98a	ro75	ro75	5t60	5t60	d04i	d04i
as0i	as0i	fw94	fw94	09n3	09m3	t3i0	t3i0
gf4i	gf4l	rfe0	rfeo	2rfk	2rfk	mda9	mda9
r39k	r39k	d39j	d39j	e20l	e20l	a76v	a76v
ays4	ays4	34tr	34tr	30ri	30ri	b9f7	b9t7
frw9	frw9	vaj3	vak3	3rfa	3rfa	h4k7	h4k7
4t9j	4l9j	30fm	30fm	fa0a	fe0a	4rj9	4rj9
id87	id87	w93k	w03k	da45	da45	m6v4	m6v4
4afa	4afa	cda9	cda9	p6la	p6la	z9ja	z9ja
dvd9	dud9	034r	034r	rf3m	rf3n	x0kp	x0kp
vas9	vas9	4tg4	4tg4	0dfi	0dfi	3r0i	3r0l
r38y	r38y	3r8h	3r8h	4gf8	4gf8	m9y7	n9y7
4t9i	4j9i	56y0	56y0	da0c	da0c	6f90	6f90
3e8a	3e8a	5tgb	5tbg	cw3o	cu3o	0k7r	0k7r
v3b9	v3b9	g402	g402	sa0k	sa0k	er6f	er6f
mx38	mx38	d3h8	d3h8	k7g4	k7g4	qt56	tq56
3r9j	3r9j	39rj	39rl	3fr0	3fr0	0iky	0iky
o02u	0o2u	30de	30de	t75i	t75l	m98t	m98t
sqy8	sqy8	g30w	g30w	69jh	69jh	u9da	u9da

Look at the four pairs of numerical digits. Circle or highlight the combination pair that **does not** match.

Sheet 2

t3u9	t3u9	58yh	58yh	w43u	w43u	c3m9	c3m9
ti30	ti30	ki90	ki90	9iy7	9yi7	bcv8	bcv8
dau8	dua8	y78d	u78d	6rda	6rda	3reh	3reh
da9f	da9f	dahj	dahj	0jh5	0jh5	fr39	fr93
hg8s	hg8s	q3j8	q8j8	ef6h	fe6h	ghj8	jgh8
s98y	s89y	34r9	34r9	b98g	b98g	f78y	f78y
6trm	6trm	dd7k	dd7k	u72y	u72y	diy4	diy4
m976	m976	fa8y	fa8y	t7tj	t7tj	r3j8	r3j8
d59m	d59m	vb49	vb49	v4h9	v4h9	h48h	h48h
54y0	54y0	4tg4	4tg4	45r8	45r8	4ty9	4ty6
gh43	gh34	hj60	hl60	76d6	76b6	df74	df74
y409	y409	dn57	dn57	o87g	o87g	4t0m	4t0m
yr3r	yr3r	593i	593i	gt7j	gt7j	4tk7	4tk7
34a0	34a0	3k5b	3k5d	vh34	v3h4	3nh6	3nh6
mn7s	mn7s	g9s6	g9s6	k6l4	k6l4	a89g	a89j
df3g	bf3g	9l6j	9l6j	lia8	lia8	h9bv	h9bv
4t8u	4t8u	ad7f	a7df	j86f	j86f	69if	69if
w30k	w03k	f86m	f86m	5d8l	5d8l	9g4m	9g4m
0l8j	0l8j	g7kl	g7kl	9k7d	9k7d	t38h	t38h
00o8	00o8	7ka8	7ka8	mx38	mx83	d39j	j39d
8yh6	8yh6	56dj	56dj	g40y	g40y	3tr9	3tr9
7g6d	7g6d	9k7d	9k7d	49jf	49jf	f8m6	f3m6
9k7g	9k7g	9rib	9crib	y0ma	y0ma	a6g8	a6g8
6f60	6f90	vma8	vma8	a89t	a98t	lg93	lg93
l085	l085	3ey4	3ye4	c39m	a39m	m6gs	m6gs
f46y	f46y	0mk8	0mk8	4t9j	4t9j	30d8	30d8
2w5j	2w5j	t8j3	t8j3	f3qp	f3qp	8d6j	86dj
6j8l	6l8j	c7n9	c7n9	3r9i	3r9i	0c62	0c62

Look at the four pairs of numerical digits. Circle or highlight the combination pair that **does not** match.

Sheet 3

4gt8h	4gt8h	a5f8m	a5f8m	g4hak	g4hak	2w9m8	2w9m8
t4r35	t4r35	gf94k	gf94k	0ala6	0aal6	93ka7	93ka7
9c4j3	9a4j3	4g9ja	4j9ja	f0m7h	f0m7h	0m37a	0m37a
30d3k	30d3k	40wpd	40wpd	39jfa	39jfa	48r3a	48r3e
t34a4	t34a4	a5c8m	a5c8m	3r7u9	3r7u9	23e6a	23e6a
0my7a	0my7a	49gf6	49gf6	r3ua6	r3ua6	95ma0	95ma0
49tay	94tay	d9ma0	9dma0	0m637	0n637	8yt3a	8yt3a
c78ma	c78ma	s9du3	s9du3	v4na5	v4na5	a8tke	a8kte
vg49m	vg49m	74mj9	74mj9	3r8ja	3r8ja	vg4ma	vg4ma
ad8j7	ad8j7	46dl8	46ld8	s98ya	s98ay	9fha7	9fha7
dmwoa	dmowa	a6m7s	a6m7s	0m6a7	0m6a7	59md7	59nd7
bfe9k	bfe9k	c7sn9	c7sn9	49kas	49kas	a9ja6	a9ja6
t3y9k	t3y9k	hg49m	gh49m	23d6g	23d6g	g48ja	g48ja
lp9a8	lp9a8	34rf9h	34rf9h	9m8g5	9m8g5	34r9k	34r9k
a8n90	a8n09	38rga	38rga	3r7gn	3r7gu	94u5j	94u5j
0aj6f	0aj6f	9k8ya	9k8ya	39fh0	39fh0	45ty9	45yt9
vb47e	vb47e	y48au	y48au	g8ujf	g8ujf	p8yat	p8tay
df93k	df93k	0l8ta	ol8ta	9ky58	9ky58	afsj8	afsj8
0lkq7	0lkq7	9kam4	9kam4	30k7t	30k7t	da85j	da85j
a9uh0	a9hu0	d0k5a	d0k5a	7kv47	7vk47	b9f6a	b9f6a
k908a	k908a	78yt4	78yt4	9iu8t	9iu8t	g49ik	g49ik
00o7a	o0o7a	l7ewa	l7ewa	p09q7	p09q7	c4ja8	c4ja8
a6td9	a6td9	0oam4	o0am4	q8r76	q8r67	qo28a	go28a
bvm8a	bvm8a	t348a	t348a	v8d6a	v8d6a	a9lac	a9lac
0ot48	0ot48	j874a	j874a	23r3k	23r3k	8v7a6	8v7a6
e5mi5	e5mi5	a9kl3	a9k3l	r3mk4	r3km4	a8r6a	a8r6a
594ka	594ak	lel39	lel39	9fm4a	9fm4a	0lo7d	olo7d
9obm5	9obm5	ut47a	ut47a	9ub7a	9ub7a	d7c9n	d7c9n

Look at the four pairs of numerical digits. Circle or highlight the combination pair that **does not** match.

Sheet 4

94f8h	94f8h	w8fr7	w8fr7	5y0a8	5y0a8	4r7a0	4r7a0
3r7ah	3r7ah	d7yms	d7yms	a8n03	an803	p9m7d	p9m7d
2me38	2em38	8v7b6	8v76b	r49j8	r49j8	s8f9h	s8f9f
e7r9b	e7r9b	n7f5a	n7f5a	0old7	0old7	bn9d7	bn9d7
8u7t6	8u7t6	y74ja	y74ja	q4r7y	q4r7y	s56g8	s56g8
q5f79	q5f79	a8wla	a8lwa	y9n3d	y9n3d	8g7d5	8g7d5
b9ma8	b9ma8	o08ar	o08ar	cv4ma	cv4am	47mf9	47mf9
9uiaj	9iuaj	385n7	385n7	b8amf	b8amf	27d0h	27dho
45t8u	45t8u	p0i98	p0i98	t934m	t934m	5r8u0	5r8u0
a9u7t	a9u7t	u876t	u876t	a8ulf	a8ulf	0l8ut	0l8tu
y76t9	u76t9	6tiqm	6tqim	mc8dg	mc8gd	a7ymi	a7ymi
89v8d	89v8d	m8ak5	m8ak5	c9ja5	c9ja5	7y5re	7y5re
q4r67	q4r67	45eru	45eru	9ikt7	9ikt7	yu59m	yu59m
78u6t	78u6t	9ki7t	9ki7t	3r03o	3r03o	4t9ua	4t9ua
8kk6a	8kk6a	8y6ra	8y6ar	e8sy7	easy7	9k8yg	9k8gy
7ahag	7haag	19mk6	19mk6	t48ua	t48ua	r38nc	r38nc
t48ua	t48ua	h57yq	h57yq	t47yi	t47yi	e239k	e239k
9k4y7	9k4y7	q87ek	q87ek	p0o8u	p0o8u	asy9n	asy9n
we7ya	we7ya	e7rol	e7rol	a7ydn	7aydn	dadhy	daddy
9mk8h	9nk8h	g89j4	g98j4	27ehf	27ehf	sd8uf	sd8uf
23m7d	23m7d	t4yay	t4yay	u8e3i	u8e3i	4t84u	4t84u
jhd3a	jhd3a	qsu82	qsu82	s9ai2	s9ai2	37an5	37an5
939ad	993ad	8de2u	8de2u	29iam	92iam	9b7aj	b97aj
8fr3j	8fr3j	8uj3a	8vj3a	e9am2	e9am2	d8uak	d8uak
il08t	il08t	yr73a	yr73a	t48ua	t48ua	5y95k	5y95k
t4i9e	t4i9e	d23ma	d23ma	23eka	23eka	t934j	t934l
e29ua	e29ua	a8hr3	a8hr8	xs9k3	xs93k	d89wu	d89wu
mf39a	fm39a	e93ja	e93ja	z8ja5	z8ja5	as8u3	as8u3

Look at the four pairs of numerical digits. Circle or highlight the combination pair that **does not** match.

Sheet 5

47yt48	47yt48	h7k9d5	h7k9d5	i9l0k9	i9l0k9	345tua	345tua
t4uam3	t4uam3	cm39ha	cm39ha	d83uai	d83uai	349ak9	349ak9
t39iai	t39iai	f39ajr	f39arj	sd3iap	sd3iap	as8u37	as8u37
43aeu3	43eau3	349aj4	349aj4	a9idam	a9iadm	fk9a83	kf9a83

yr36u8	yr36u8	59tjma	59tjma	t48amo	t48amo	xzu78a	xzu78a
t4ju9a	t4ju9a	0kl8u8	0kl8u8	lo9jd7	io9jd7	zi9km6	zi9km6
f39mai	f39mia	89u7t6	89v7t6	dy8jr3	dy8jr3	sak95a	sak95a
bmia94	bmia94	65b8k0	65b8k0	r3k9ar	r3k9ar	dkw95o	wkd95o

u6y564	u6y564	j84jfh	j84jfh	v5j7o8	v5j708	fj4j6o	fj4j6o
r03o87	r03o87	h834k3	h834k3	ihy54r	ihy54r	o8u646	o8u646
t48umg	t48mug	e3iu9a	e3iu9a	j6g4ae	j6g4ae	c4as78	c4as87
l0f48a	l0f48a	u8r3k8	8ur3k8	k75fd5	k75fd5	n6b546	n6b546

y4u8a0	y4u8a0	8v4m83	8v4m83	15rq17	15rg17	45tui4	45tui4
94ri8u	94ri8u	389ruf	389ruf	9ki47d	9ki47d	r45945	r45945
6tr9n3	6tr6n3	g49is4	g49is4	r398ur	r398ur	cm8t57	mc8t57
2746n4	2746n4	r49ia7	r94ia7	0lo84j	0lo84j	t4u49r	t4u49r

vm48u8	vm48u3	cm388u	cm388u	35tru9	35tru9	4598r4	4598r4
r348ur	r348ur	598gtk	598gtk	649frk	649frk	978t6e	978t6e
r93ia0	r93ia0	48rk4m	48kr4m	e2u9j3	2eu9j3	867yt9	867ty9
pl4idj	pl4idj	09g8m4	09g8m4	6m8d6d	6m8d6d	248a78	248a78

4t87u4	4t87u4	9445r3	9445r3	358fr4	358fr4	34dh3a	34bh3a
49t49i	49t49i	98jr47	98jr47	9573c8	9573c8	39k57a	39k57a
et5i95	et5i95	3748i6	3748i6	87dh76	78dh76	5na7m5	5na7m5
3958r9	3985r9	278eu3	278ue3	098dy8	098dy8	983ma8	983ma8

r39a8a	r39a0a	469ut4	469ut4	459dak	459dak	t49iak	t49iak
n697a6	n697a6	86j48a	68j48a	r3yu8a	r3yu8a	dfk49a	dfk49a
96ma95	96ma95	78ash7	78ash7	u48ah2	v48ah2	fm48ua	fm48ua
plcv48	plcv48	34e8a3	34e8a3	js82a8	js82a8	458f4m	458f4n

Look at the four pairs of numerical digits. Circle or highlight the combination pair that **does not** match.

Sheet 6

4tt47	4tt47	23e8a	23e8a	4t90i	4t90i	457a6	457a6
t69i4	t69i4	49tia	49tia	f48ua	f84ua	94o93	94o93
df9ua	df9va	94y5p	94j5p	648aj	648aj	2n848	2o848
gf49u	gf49u	9isak	9isak	54ma7	54ma7	i4370	i4370

t8u4a	t8v4a	tr4u8	tr48u	k8g4h	k8g4h	349ua	349ua
f49ur	f49ur	werop	werop	f4j8a	f4ja8	37fh4	37hf4
u4u09	u4u09	3539f	3539f	nc38a	nc38a	2b3m6	2b3m6
k89t4	k89t4	j8g4a	j8g4a	9ujd3	9ujd3	3nm8a	3nm8a

8ut4s	3ut4s	i478g	i478g
496f4	496f4	gj348	gj348
9k8ya	9k8ya	ngf84	gnf84
78a9p	78a9p	bh48a	bh48a

ANSWERS TO TEST 2

Sheet 1

j07r	j07r	mv39	mv93	g39j	g39j	p20s	p20s
l086	i086	ru28	ru28	e2k0	e2k0	w95r	w95r
3e5d	3e5d	otr4	otr4	30ri	30ir	ccv4	cav4
u90f	u90f	03w2	03w2	e22f	e22f	fj3a	fj3a
qp20	pq20	hg94	hg94	34r9	34r9	ioa8	ioa8
cme3	cme3	lldk	lldk	e03i	e03i	yo65	yo65
eo03	eo03	30dp	3odp	f3k0	f3k0	v49f	u49f
r30i	r30i	wp20	wp20	mn03	nn03	g349	g349
fl02	fl02	daj5	daj5	fal4	fal4	3r0f	r30f
m98a	m98a	ro75	ro75	5t60	5t60	d04i	d04i
as0i	as0i	fw94	fw94	09n3	09m3	t3i0	t3i0
gf4i	gf4l	rfe0	rfeo	2rfk	2rfk	mda9	mda9
r39k	r39k	d39j	d39j	e20l	e20l	a76v	a76v
ays4	ays4	34tr	34tr	30ri	30ri	b9f7	b9t7
frw9	frw9	vaj3	vak3	3rfa	3rfa	h4k7	h4k7
4t9j	4l9j	30fm	30fm	fa0a	fe0a	4rj9	4rj9
id87	id87	w93k	w03k	da45	da45	m6v4	m6v4
4afa	4afa	cda9	cda9	p6la	p6la	z9ja	z9ja
dvd9	dud9	034r	034r	rf3m	rf3n	x0kp	x0kp
vas9	vas9	4tg4	4tg4	0dfi	0dfi	3r0i	3r0l
r38y	r38y	3r8h	3r8h	4gf8	4gf8	m9y7	n9y7
4t9i	4j9i	56y0	56y0	da0c	da0c	6f90	6f90
3e8a	3e8a	5tgb	5tbg	cw3o	cu3o	0k7r	0k7r
v3b9	v3b9	g402	g402	sa0k	sa0k	er6f	er6f
mx38	mx38	d3h8	d3h8	k7g4	k7g4	qt56	tq56
3r9j	3r9j	39rj	39rl	3fr0	3fr0	0iky	0iky
o02u	0o2u	30de	30de	t75i	t75l	m98t	m98t
sqy8	sqy8	g30w	g30w	69jh	69jh	u9da	u9da

Sheet 2

t3u9	t3u9	58yh	58yh	w43u	w43u	c3m9	c3m9
ti30	ti30	ki90	ki90	9iy7	9yi7	bcv8	bcv8
dau8	dua8	y78d	u78d	6rda	6rda	3reh	3reh
da9f	da9f	dahj	dahj	0jh5	0jh5	fr39	fr93
hg8s	hg8s	q3j8	q8j8	ef6h	fe6h	ghj8	jgh8
s98y	s89y	34r9	34r9	b98g	b98g	f78y	f78y
6trm	6trm	dd7k	dd7k	u72y	u72y	diy4	diy4
m976	m976	fa8y	fa8y	t7tj	t7tj	r3j8	r3j8
d59m	d59m	vb49	vb49	v4h9	v4h9	h48h	h48h
54y0	54y0	4tg4	4tg4	45r8	45r8	4ty9	4ty6
gh43	gh34	hj60	hl60	76d6	76b6	df74	df74
y409	y409	dn57	dn57	o87g	o87g	4t0m	4t0m
yr3r	yr3r	593i	593i	gt7j	gt7j	4tk7	4tk7
34a0	34a0	3k5b	3k5d	vh34	v3h4	3nh6	3nh6
mn7s	mn7s	g9s6	g9s6	k6l4	k6l4	a89g	a89j
df3g	bf3g	9l6j	9l6j	lia8	lia8	h9bv	h9bv
4t8u	4t8u	ad7f	a7df	j86f	j86f	69if	69if
w30k	w03k	f86m	f86m	5d8l	5d8l	9g4m	9g4m
0l8j	0l8j	g7kl	g7kl	9k7d	9k7d	t38h	t38h
00o8	00o8	7ka8	7ka8	mx38	mx83	d39j	j39d
8yh6	8yh6	56dj	56dj	g40y	g40y	3tr9	3tr9
7g6d	7g6d	9k7d	9k7d	49jf	49jf	f8m6	f3m6
9k7g	9k7g	9rib	9crib	y0ma	y0ma	a6g8	a6g8
6f60	6f90	vma8	vma8	a89t	a98t	lg93	lg93
l085	l085	3ey4	3ye4	c39m	a39m	m6gs	m6gs
f46y	f46y	0mk8	0mk8	4t9j	4t9j	30d8	30d8
2w5j	2w5j	t8j3	t8j3	f3qp	f3qp	8d6j	86dj
6j8l	6l8j	c7n9	c7n9	3r9i	3r9i	0c62	0c62

Sheet 3

4gt8h	4gt8h	a5f8m	a5f8m	g4hak	g4hak	2w9m8	2w9m8
t4r35	t4r35	gf94k	gf94k	0ala6	0aal6	93ka7	93ka7
9c4j3	9a4j3	4g9ja	4j9ja	f0m7h	f0m7h	0m37a	0m37a
30d3k	30d3k	40wpd	40wpd	39jfa	39jfa	48r3a	48r3e

t34a4	t34a4	a5c8m	a5c8m	3r7u9	3r7u9	23e6a	23e6a
0my7a	0my7a	49gf6	49gf6	r3ua6	r3ua6	95ma0	95ma0
49tay	94tay	d9ma0	9dma0	0m637	0n637	8yt3a	8yt3a
c78ma	c78ma	s9du3	s9du3	v4na5	v4na5	a8tke	a8kte

vg49m	vg49m	74mj9	74mj9	3r8ja	3r8ja	vg4ma	vg4ma
ad8j7	ad8j7	46dl8	46ld8	s98ya	s98ay	9fha7	9fha7
dmwoa	dmowa	a6m7s	a6m7s	0m6a7	0m6a7	59md7	59nd7
bfe9k	bfe9k	c7sn9	c7sn9	49kas	49kas	a9ja6	a9ja6

t3y9k	t3y9k	hg49m	gh49m	23d6g	23d6g	g48ja	g48ja
lp9a8	lp9a8	34rf9h	34rf9h	9m8g5	9m8g5	34r9k	34r9k
a8n90	a8n09	38rga	38rga	3r7gn	3r7gu	94u5j	94u5j
0aj6f	0aj6f	9k8ya	9k8ya	39fh0	39fh0	45ty9	45yt9

vb47e	vb47e	y48au	y48au	g8ujf	g8ujf	p8yat	p8tay
df93k	df93k	0l8ta	ol8ta	9ky58	9ky58	afsj8	afsj8
0lkq7	0lkq7	9kam4	9kam4	30k7t	30k7t	da85j	da85j
a9uh0	a9hu0	d0k5a	d0k5a	7kv47	7vk47	b9f6a	b9f6a

k908a	k908a	78yt4	78yt4	9iu8t	9iu8t	g49ik	g49ik
00o7a	o0o7a	l7ewa	l7ewa	p09q7	p09q7	c4ja8	c4ja8
a6td9	a6td9	0oam4	o0am4	q8r76	q8r67	qo28a	go28a
bvm8a	bvm8a	t348a	t348a	v8d6a	v8d6a	a9lac	a9lac

0ot48	0ot48	j874a	j874a	23r3k	23r3k	8v7a6	8v7a6
e5mi5	e5mi5	a9kl3	a9k3l	r3mk4	r3km4	a8r6a	a8r6a
594ka	594ak	lel39	lel39	9fm4a	9fm4a	0lo7d	olo7d
9obm5	9obm5	ut47a	ut47a	9ub7a	9ub7a	d7c9n	d7c9n

Sheet 4

94f8h	94f8h	w8fr7	w8fr7	5y0a8	5y0a8	4r7a0	4r7a0
3r7ah	3r7ah	d7yms	d7yms	a8n03	an803	p9m7d	p9m7d
2me38	2em38	8v7b6	8v76b	r49j8	r49j8	s8f9h	s8f9f
e7r9b	e7r9b	n7f5a	n7f5a	0old7	0old7	bn9d7	bn9d7
8u7t6	8u7t6	y74ja	y74ja	q4r7y	q4r7y	s56g8	s56g8
q5f79	q5f79	a8wla	a8lwa	y9n3d	y9n3d	8g7d5	8g7d5
b9ma8	b9ma8	o08ar	o08ar	cv4ma	cv4am	47mf9	47mf9
9uiaj	9iuaj	385n7	385n7	b8amf	b8amf	27d0h	27dho
45t8u	45t8u	p0i98	p0i98	t934m	t934m	5r8u0	5r8u0
a9u7t	a9u7t	u876t	u876t	a8ulf	a8ulf	0l8ut	0l8tu
y76t9	u76t9	6tiqm	6tqim	mc8dg	mc8gd	a7ymi	a7ymi
89v8d	89v8d	m8ak5	m8ak5	c9ja5	c9ja5	7y5re	7y5re
q4r67	q4r67	45eru	45eru	9ikt7	9ikt7	yu59m	yu59m
78u6t	78u6t	9ki7t	9ki7t	3r03o	3r03o	4t9ua	4t9ua
8kk6a	8kk6a	8y6ra	8y6ar	e8sy7	easy7	9k8yg	9k8gy
7ahag	7haag	19mk6	19mk6	t48ua	t48ua	r38nc	r38nc
t48ua	t48ua	h57yq	h57yq	t47yi	t47yi	e239k	e239k
9k4y7	9k4y7	q87ek	q87ek	p0o8u	p0o8u	asy9n	asy9n
we7ya	we7ya	e7rol	e7rol	a7ydn	7aydn	dadhy	daddy
9mk8h	9nk8h	g89j4	g98j4	27ehf	27ehf	sd8uf	sd8uf
23m7d	23m7d	t4yay	t4yay	u8e3i	u8e3i	4t84u	4t84u
jhd3a	jhd3a	qsu82	qsu82	s9ai2	s9ai2	37an5	37an5
939ad	993ad	8de2u	8de2u	29iam	92iam	9b7aj	b97aj
8fr3j	8fr3j	8uj3a	8vj3a	e9am2	e9am2	d8uak	d8uak
il08t	il08t	yr73a	yr73a	t48ua	t48ua	5y95k	5y95k
t4i9e	t4i9e	d23ma	d23ma	23eka	23eka	t934j	t934l
e29ua	e29ua	a8hr3	a8hr8	xs9k3	xs93k	d89wu	d89wu
mf39a	fm39a	e93ja	e93ja	z8ja5	z8ja5	as8u3	as8u3

Sheet 5

47yt48	47yt48	h7k9d5	h7k9d5	i9l0k9	i9l0k9	345tua	345tua
t4uam3	t4uam3	cm39ha	cm39ha	d83uai	d83uai	349ak9	349ak9
t39iai	t39iai	f39ajr	f39arj	sd3iap	sd3iap	as8u37	as8u37
43aeu3	43eau3	349aj4	349aj4	a9idam	a9iadm	fk9a83	kf9a83

yr36u8	yr36u8	59tjma	59tjma	t48amo	t48amo	xzu78a	xzu78a
t4ju9a	t4ju9a	0kl8u8	0kl8u8	lo9jd7	io9jd7	zi9km6	zi9km6
f39mai	f39mia	89u7t6	89v7t6	dy8jr3	dy8jr3	sak95a	sak95a
bmia94	bmia94	65b8k0	65b8k0	r3k9ar	r3k9ar	dkw95o	wkd95o

u6y564	u6y564	j84jfh	j84jfh	v5j7o8	v5j7o8	fj4j6o	fj4j6o
r03o87	r03o87	h834k3	h834k3	ihy54r	ihy54r	o8u646	o8u646
t48umg	t48mug	e3iu9a	e3iu9a	j6g4ae	j6g4ae	c4as78	c4as87
l0f48a	l0f48a	u8r3k8	8ur3k8	k75fd5	k75fd5	n6b546	n6b546

y4u8a0	y4u8a0	8v4m83	8v4m83	15rq17	15rg17	45tui4	45tui4
94ri8u	94ri8u	389ruf	389ruf	9ki47d	9ki47d	r45945	r45945
6tr9n3	6tr6n3	g49is4	g49is4	r398ur	r398ur	cm8t57	mc8t57
2746n4	2746n4	r49ia7	r94ia7	0lo84j	0lo84j	t4u49r	t4u49r

vm48u8	vm48u3	cm388u	cm388u	35tru9	35tru9	4598r4	4598r4
r348ur	r348ur	598gtk	598gtk	649frk	649frk	978t6e	978t6e
r93ia0	r93ia0	48rk4m	48kr4m	e2u9j3	2eu9j3	867yt9	867ty9
pl4idj	pl4idj	09g8m4	09g8m4	6m8d6d	6m8d6d	248a78	248a78

4t87u4	4t87u4	9445r3	9445r3	358fr4	358fr4	34dh3a	34bh3a
49t49i	49t49i	98jr47	98jr47	9573c8	9573c8	39k57a	39k57a
et5i95	et5i95	3748i6	3748i6	87dh76	78dh76	5na7m5	5na7m5
3958r9	3985r9	278eu3	278ue3	098dy8	098dy8	983ma8	983ma8

r39a8a	r39a0a	469ut4	469ut4	459dak	459dak	t49iak	t49iak
n697a6	n697a6	86j48a	68j48a	r3yu8a	r3yu8a	dfk49a	dfk49a
96ma95	96ma95	78ash7	78ash7	u48ah2	v48ah2	fm48ua	fm48ua
plcv48	plcv48	34e8a3	34e8a3	js82a8	js82a8	458f4m	458f4n

Sheet 6

4tt47	4tt47	23e8a	23e8a	4t90i	4t90i	457a6	457a6
t69i4	t69i4	49tia	49tia	f48ua	f84ua	94o93	94o93
df9ua	df9va	94y5p	94j5p	648aj	648aj	2n848	2o848
gf49u	gf49u	9isak	9isak	54ma7	54ma7	i4370	i4370
t8u4a	t8v4a	tr4u8	tr48u	k8g4h	k8g4h	349ua	349ua
f49ur	f49ur	werop	werop	f4j8a	f4ja8	37fh4	37hf4
u4u09	u4u09	3539f	3539f	nc38a	nc38a	2b3m6	2b3m6
k89t4	k89t4	j8g4a	j8g4a	9ujd3	9ujd3	3nm8a	3nm8a
8ut4s	3ut4s	i478g	i478g				
496f4	496f4	gj348	gj348				
9k8ya	9k8ya	ngf84	gnf84				
78a9p	78a9p	bh48a	bh48a				

CHAPTER FIVE
DOTS CONCENTRATION TEST (DCT)

The Dots Concentration Test (DCT) is a test that assesses your ability to concentrate for long periods of time, and is probably the hardest skill to master in psychometric testing. It is the one test that most people fail and this is mainly due to a lack of preparation. Many candidates turn up to take the test without any prior knowledge of how it works and what is expected of them.

The test is designed to assess your ability to concentrate whilst performing tasks at high speed. The test will be carried out either with a pen and paper, or a computer and a computer screen. Whichever test you undertake, you will be presented with five pages or screens that each contains 25 columns. Each of the columns contains boxes with patterns of dots. Your task is to work quickly and accurately through each column, from left to right, identifying boxes of 4 dots only.

You are allowed two minutes only per sheet and, once the two minutes are up, you are told to move onto the next page regardless of whether you have completed it or not. The test requires ten minutes of solid concentration.

Take a look at the following row of dots:

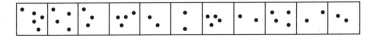

You will notice that the 2nd, 4th, 7th and 9th boxes each contain 4 dots. If you were taking the paper and pencil based version of the test, you would mark the boxes that contain 4 dots as follows:

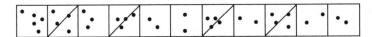

You will notice that I have placed a single diagonal line through each of the boxes that contains 4 dots.

If you are required to undertake the computer based version of the test then you will be required to use the keys on the keyboard as follows:

    You will use this key to move from left to right across the screen.

    You will use this key to mark each box that contains 4 dots.

    You will use this key to move back in order to correct any mistakes.

On the following pages I have provided you with sample concentration tests. During the first set of five concentration tests you are required to locate specific letters and/or numbers that are contained within rows and columns. Full instructions are provided at the start of each test.

You will be required to search for groups of 4 dots in rows and columns of boxes. Once again, full instructions are provided.

SAMPLE CONCENTRATION TEST 1

Cross out the letter 'F' (upper case) in each row. Write down the total number that you cross out in each row in the box provided at the end of each row. You have 60 seconds to complete the test.

#															
1.	Q	r	R	g	y	U	h	J	R	j	R	k	L	B	n	
2.	R	R	R	v	B	n	M	U	u	d	f	O	p	T	R	
3.	C	x	X	F	R	G	t	p	A	R	f	V	R	y	U	
4.	Q	R	R	t	G	N	H	J	r	r	F	P	F	R	r	
5.	Q	a	Z	x	R	t	I	o	M	B	R	D	x	A	S	
6.	R	s	a	A	e	E	R	C	Y	U	r	j	P	o	R	
7.	T	R	r	P	F	r	S	N	b	V	c	F	F	R	R	
8.	G	v	R	r	R	y	R	P	R	r	D	e	E	R	F	
9.	T	R	K	P	o	u	b	g	t	m	R	r	X	r	R	
10.	C	B	n	h	j	Y	I	p	R	R	R	r	R	C	d	
11.	R	R	r	Y	u	B	v	M	n	h	K	j	R	E	R	
12.	A	W	r	E	R	f	p	U	I	H	R	y	U	B	R	
13.	R	r	Q	q	B	G	R	t	Q	w	E	F	T	y	R	
14.	T	R	A	I	N	D	P	I	V	E	R	D	T	y	S	
15.	d	x	z	Z	R	n	K	i	i	R	r	R	O	p	o	
16.	Q	R	r	E	D	D	e	w	K	i	I	O	P	R	R	
17.	H	O	w	B	e	E	R	r	R	R	V	R	H	j	R	
18.	K	j	u	U	Y	i	Y	r	R	R	D	X	z	q	Q	
19.	P	y	g	h	j	I	r	t	r	e	R	e	R	q	Z	
20.	B	h	B	h	r	r	R	r	N	B	H	y	Y	R	F	

SAMPLE CONCENTRATION TEST 2

Cross out the letter 'Y' (upper case). Write down the total number that you cross out in each row in the box provided at the end of each row. You have 60 seconds to complete the test.

1.	o	O	t	Q	w	q	O	o	A	B	u	U	o	o	O	
2.	O	o	g	Y	t	B	c	C	c	O	o	o	o	D	w	
3.	B	o	O	g	a	s	S	q	Q	t	Q	q	O	o	G	
4.	I	L	N	h	U	u	O	o	H	y	t	R	o	O	o	
5.	G	V	v	R	t	Y	o	o	P	i	O	O	o	O	R	
6.	G	t	y	U	J	P	p	O	o	D	d	O	o	S	Q	
7.	O	o	O	o	o	o	Y	t	Y	q	Q	q	o	c	c	
8.	I	u	V	c	c	F	r	d	w	H	y	h	u	o	o	
9.	Y	o	o	U	o	O	O	y	D	e	q	A	q	O	o	
10.	R	r	t	o	u	y	G	b	t	r	e	o	o	o	P	
11.	o	O	c	o	d	d	D	O	c	c	O	o	o	d	R	
12.	B	v	c	f	R	o	y	f	D	r	d	r	a	A	a	
13.	F	t	t	t	d	r	e	o	o	p	u	o	Q	t	r	
14.	F	g	r	t	y	N	H	N	h	o	p	O	o	I	y	
15.	T	r	e	d	w	o	u	i	y	F	c	r	D	e	W	
16.	o	o	O	o	p	O	u	i	S	t	d	r	s	S	O	
17.	I	o	O	A	a	a	c	C	c	g	o	o	o	R	t	
18.	G	g	g	g	o	t	f	d	r	t	u	u	o	o	j	
19.	Q	c	v	b	g	t	y	u	O	o	O	o	G	y	c	
20.	K	I	o	i	u	y	t	r	e	o	u	y	o	j	h	

SAMPLE CONCENTRATION TEST 3

Cross out the letters 'g' (lower case) and 'W' (upper case). Search for both of these letters at the same time. Write down the total combined number that you cross out in each row in the box provided at the end of each row. You have 60 seconds to complete the test.

1.	v	W	w	V	e	w	h	j	U	i	X	x	W	w	v
2.	V	u	U	w	G	t	y	u	W	w	V	v	W	o	o
3.	W	W	V	V	v	v	w	w	y	u	i	p	v	W	W
4.	V	g	h	j	K	O	p	t	Y	V	v	W	W	w	V
5.	Y	U	u	u	v	v	W	M	m	w	e	V	v	N	n
6.	q	q	Q	G	g	H	Y	u	i	R	T	y	V	w	v
7.	V	y	u	Y	u	o	p	N	h	j	W	w	V	V	v
8.	t	y	m	k	m	N	b	C	x	W	w	V	v	b	v
9.	O	o	V	v	f	g	h	j	k	n	h	N	h	V	X
10.	T	V	v	X	c	d	W	w	W	v	V	v	f	r	p
11.	V	V	v	w	W	w	v	V	v	W	w	g	y	Y	v
12.	R	t	y	u	i	B	g	v	f	r	D	r	Q	w	W
13.	R	t	y	V	c	V	c	v	f	r	W	w	W	w	V
14.	G	y	u	i	O	p	R	t	y	E	w	V	V	v	W
15.	Y	Y	y	Y	X	v	W	W	w	w	r	t	y	u	v
16.	W	w	w	v	t	u	i	n	h	v	V	w	W	w	f
17.	r	t	y	y	u	i	V	b	n	h	g	w	w	W	w
18.	i	o	q	w	S	S	X	W	V	Z	z	V	v	W	y
19.	P	o	Y	u	i	V	v	X	w	W	w	R	t	R	y
20.	y	u	V	x	s	t	Y	u	y	W	w	C	d	V	w

SAMPLE CONCENTRATION TEST 4

Cross out the number 3 and the letter 'q' (lower case). Search for both letter and number at the same time. Write down the total combined number that you cross out in each row in the box provided at the end of each row. You have 60 seconds to complete the test.

1.	8	B	8	V	v	W	q	P	p	r	g	B	b	8	u	
2.	B	b	R	r	r	y	U	i	8	8	B	B	b	g	G	
3.	j	u	p	P	b	v	f	r	B	b	w	3	6	7	R	
4.	8	3	2	h	y	U	x	W	w	v	x	v	b	B	8	
5.	f	G	g	B	p	h	b	b	b	B	B	8	8	5	3	
6.	y	u	U	7	6	5	8	e	r	d	r	w	8	B	b	
7.	o	O	o	P	7	8	5	b	3	8	3	R	r	S	l	
8.	B	b	3	8	B	B	b	h	h	V	c	b	B	7	1	
9.	1	3	c	V	f	l	u	y	t	r	B	b	8	8	8	
10.	y	B	b	8	4	3	3	3	X	x	x	f	F	r	t	
11.	Q	q	H	b	B	b	8	B	6	3	3	2	u	B	b	
12.	G	G	g	B	b	8	3	8	3	D	d	D	l	P	p	
13.	G	b	b	8	8	6	5	4	0	L	o	P	p	P	B	
14.	3	B	b	8	3	B	B	b	3	E	e	3	8	4	P	
15.	t	Y	y	D	e	e	D	f	g	W	8	8	P	P	B	
16.	C	C	b	n	B	8	B	8	B	b	8	3	9	3	9	
17.	6	6	b	B	8	8	d	k	l	p	o	U	S	y	Y	
18.	P	p	8	F	d	D	c	C	8	B	b	8	f	F	f	
19.	8	8	C	f	z	s	W	w	R	r	T	8	3	B	b	
20.	H	y	y	b	B	8	8	8	H	H	h	D	r	e	W	

SAMPLE CONCENTRATION TEST 5

Cross out the letter 'e' (lower case) and the number '3'. Search for both letter and number at the same time. Write down the number crossed out in the box provided at the end of each row. You have 60 seconds to complete the test.

#																
1.	E	6	e	8	8	e	3	p	b	d	e	E	3	8	T	
2.	e	8	3	6	7	y	u	I	V	f	E	e	b	B	E	
3.	W	w	q	D	d	c	X	z	O	p	e	R	6	8	3	
4.	y	u	I	o	p	P	t	T	Y	e	E	3	8	6	F	
5.	g	B	4	3	2	7	8	3	e	E	3	4	E	e	3	
6.	e	3	3	e	E	d	W	q	h	j	K	8	7	N	9	
7.	3	e	E	8	B	8	3	e	E	k	K	3	e	8	7	
8.	f	C	X	b	g	t	T	r	6	8	3	4	X	d	e	
9.	3	3	3	b	8	b	e	3	E	3	8	3	4	0	1	
10.	e	E	j	H	g	b	3	E	e	3	w	b	V	v	E	
11.	8	3	B	v	C	f	v	e	8	4	3	3	3	e	v	
12.	6	7	8	v	c	D	f	3	7	8	6	E	e	e	V	
13.	e	3	e	3	E	8	E	3	e	E	3	2	8	G	g	
14.	7	y	h	n	g	f	d	e	E	4	E	e	3	D	d	
15.	k	I	L	j	h	y	V	v	8	4	2	b	V	v	E	
16.	g	Y	y	i	9	8	7	0	3	O	o	v	V	v	e	
17.	8	2	B	b	v	e	W	e	r	5	5	R	r	e	V	
18.	3	e	E	e	3	4	b	V	v	e	W	w	q	A	a	
19.	5	e	3	V	f	r	6	5	4	e	e	E	e	3	E	
20.	e	E	e	R	3	4	2	1	3	E	e	h	G	f	d	

ANSWERS TO CONCENTRATION TESTS

TEST 1

1.	0	6.	0	11.	0	16.	0
2.	0	7.	3	12.	0	17.	0
3.	1	8.	1	13.	1	18.	0
4.	2	9.	0	14.	0	19.	0
5.	0	10.	0	15.	0	20.	1

TEST 2

1.	0	6.	0	11.	0	16.	0
2.	1	7.	2	12.	0	17.	0
3.	0	8.	0	13.	0	18.	0
4.	0	9.	1	14.	0	19.	0
5.	1	10.	0	15.	0	20.	0

TEST 3

1.	2	6.	1	11.	3	16.	2
2.	2	7.	1	12.	2	17.	2
3.	4	8.	1	13.	2	18.	2
4.	3	9.	1	14.	1	19.	1
5.	1	10.	2	15.	2	20.	1

TEST 4

1.	1	6.	0	11.	3	16.	2
2.	0	7.	2	12.	2	17.	0
3.	1	8.	1	13.	0	18.	0
4.	1	9.	1	14.	4	19.	1
5.	1	10.	3	15.	0	20.	0

TEST 5

1.	5	6.	4	11.	6	16.	2
2.	3	7.	6	12.	3	17.	3
3.	2	8.	2	13.	7	18.	5
4.	2	9.	7	14.	3	19.	6
5.	6	10.	4	15.	0	20.	5

Check through your answers carefully and go back to check over the ones you got wrong.

Now move onto to the next set of Dots Concentration tests.

You have been provided just 30 seconds to complete each question.

Please note: this will generally not be sufficient time to complete each question. The reason for the strict time limit is to increase the pressure that you are placed under; something which will be prevalent during the real test.

It is very important that you work towards both speed and accuracy as the assessors will deduct marks for wild guessing and incorrect answers

You may decide to not use a time limit and work through each page separately. If you do take this option, consider breaking the tests down into either groups of 5, 10 or two sets of 25.

The answers are provided at the end of the section.

Good luck!

SAMPLE DOTS CONCENTRATION TESTS 1

Place a diagonal line across each box that contains 4 dots only. You have 30 seconds to complete the test.

Answer [   ]

SAMPLE DOTS CONCENTRATION TESTS 2

Place a diagonal line across each box that contains 4 dots only. You have 30 seconds to complete the test.

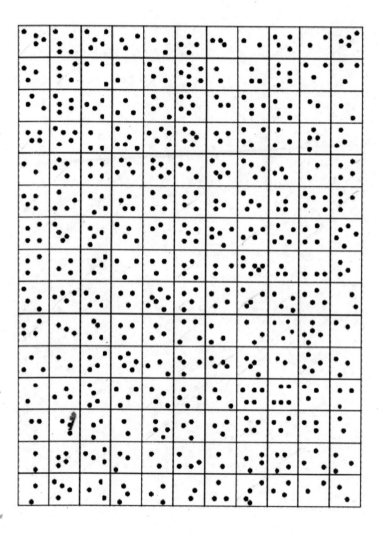

Answer

SAMPLE DOTS CONCENTRATION TESTS 3

Place a diagonal line across each box that contains 4 dots only. You have 30 seconds to complete the test.

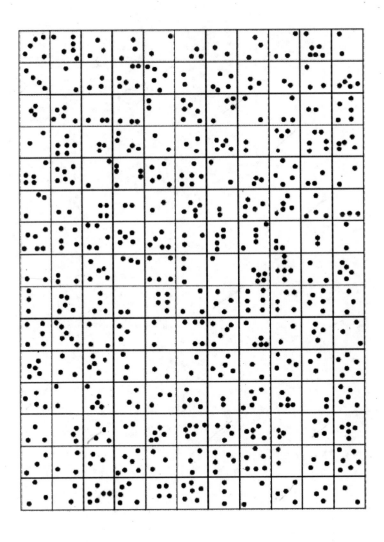

Answer

SAMPLE DOTS CONCENTRATION TESTS 4

Place a diagonal line across each box that contains 4 dots only. You have 30 seconds to complete the test.

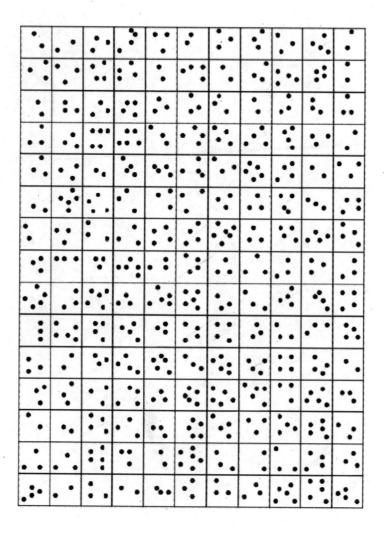

Answer

SAMPLE DOTS CONCENTRATION TESTS 5

Place a diagonal line across each box that contains 4 dots only. You have 30 seconds to complete the test.

Answer [   ]

SAMPLE DOTS CONCENTRATION TESTS 6

Place a diagonal line across each box that contains 4 dots only. You have 30 seconds to complete the test.

Answer [   ]

SAMPLE DOTS CONCENTRATION TESTS 7

Place a diagonal line across each box that contains 4 dots only. You have 30 seconds to complete the test.

Answer

SAMPLE DOTS CONCENTRATION TESTS 8

Place a diagonal line across each box that contains 4 dots only. You have 30 seconds to complete the test.

Answer

SAMPLE DOTS CONCENTRATION TESTS 9

Place a diagonal line across each box that contains 4 dots only. You have 30 seconds to complete the test.

Answer

SAMPLE DOTS CONCENTRATION TESTS 10

Place a diagonal line across each box that contains 4 dots only. You have 30 seconds to complete the test.

Answer [ ]

SAMPLE DOTS CONCENTRATION TESTS 11

Place a diagonal line across each box that contains 4 dots only. You have 30 seconds to complete the test.

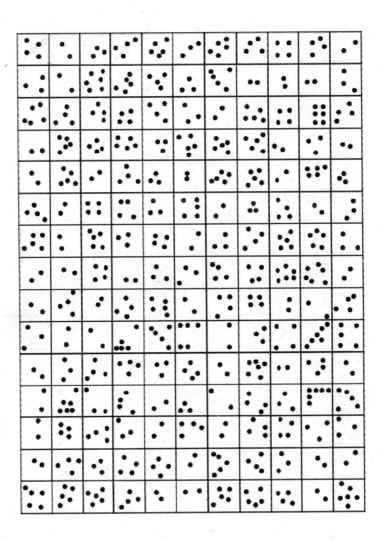

Answer

SAMPLE DOTS CONCENTRATION TESTS 12

Place a diagonal line across each box that contains 4 dots only. You have 30 seconds to complete the test.

Answer [ ]

SAMPLE DOTS CONCENTRATION TESTS 13

Place a diagonal line across each box that contains 4 dots only. You have 30 seconds to complete the test.

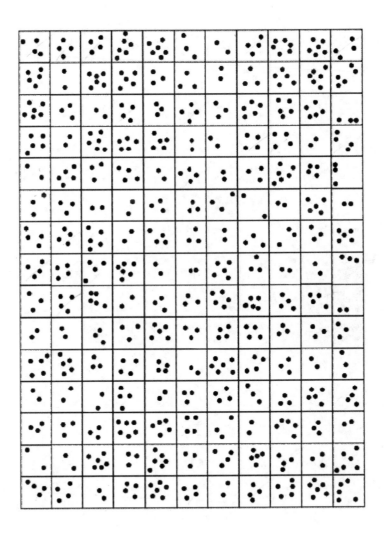

Answer

SAMPLE DOTS CONCENTRATION TEST 14

Place a diagonal line across each box that contains 4 dots only. You have 30 seconds to complete the test.

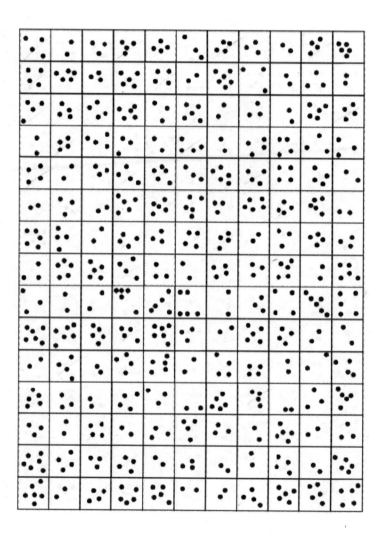

Answer

SAMPLE DOTS CONCENTRATION TEST 15

Place a diagonal line across each box that contains 4 dots only. You have 30 seconds to complete the test.

Answer

SAMPLE DOTS CONCENTRATION TEST 16

Place a diagonal line across each box that contains 4 dots only. You have 30 seconds to complete the test.

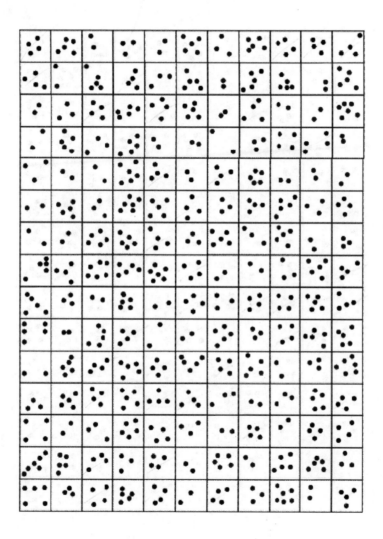

Answer

SAMPLE DOTS CONCENTRATION TEST 17

Place a diagonal line across each box that contains 4 dots only. You have 30 seconds to complete the test.

Answer [   ]

SAMPLE DOTS CONCENTRATION TEST 18

Place a diagonal line across each box that contains 4 dots only. You have 30 seconds to complete the test.

Answer [   ]

SAMPLE DOTS CONCENTRATION TEST 19

Place a diagonal line across each box that contains 4 dots only. You have 30 seconds to complete the test.

Answer

SAMPLE DOTS CONCENTRATION TEST 20

Place a diagonal line across each box that contains 4 dots only. You have 30 seconds to complete the test.

Answer

SAMPLE DOTS CONCENTRATION TEST 21 /

Place a diagonal line across each box that contains 4 dots only. You have 30 seconds to complete the test.

Answer [   ]

SAMPLE DOTS CONCENTRATION TEST 22

Place a diagonal line across each box that contains 4 dots only. You have 30 seconds to complete the test.

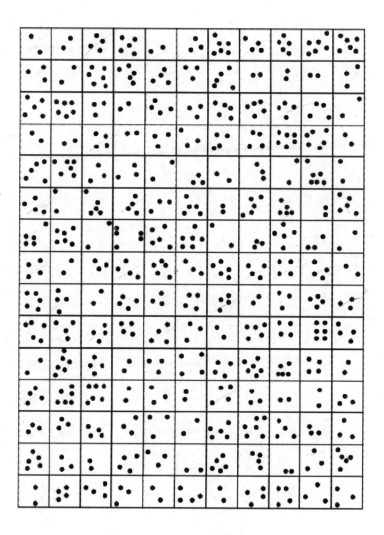

Answer [   ]

SAMPLE DOTS CONCENTRATION TEST 23

Place a diagonal line across each box that contains 4 dots only. You have 30 seconds to complete the test.

Answer [   ]

SAMPLE DOTS CONCENTRATION TEST 24

Place a diagonal line across each box that contains 4 dots only. You have 30 seconds to complete the test.

Answer

SAMPLE DOTS CONCENTRATION TEST 25

Place a diagonal line across each box that contains 4 dots only. You have 30 seconds to complete the test.

Answer [   ]

SAMPLE DOTS CONCENTRATION TEST 26

Place a diagonal line across each box that contains 4 dots only. You have 30 seconds to complete the test.

Answer [   ]

SAMPLE DOTS CONCENTRATION TEST 27

Place a diagonal line across each box that contains 4 dots only. You have 30 seconds to complete the test.

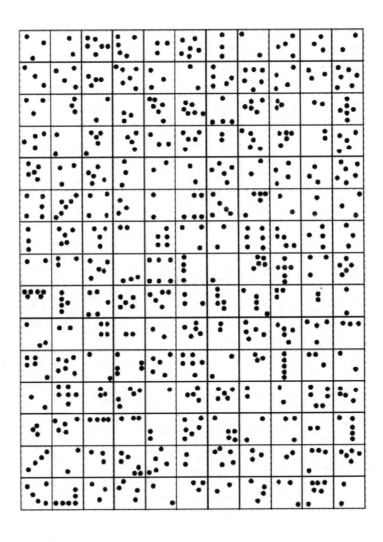

Answer [   ]

SAMPLE DOTS CONCENTRATION TEST 28

Place a diagonal line across each box that contains 4 dots only. You have 30 seconds to complete the test.

Answer [   ]

SAMPLE DOTS CONCENTRATION TEST 29

Place a diagonal line across each box that contains 4 dots only. You have 30 seconds to complete the test.

Answer

SAMPLE DOTS CONCENTRATION TEST 30

Place a diagonal line across each box that contains 4 dots only. You have 30 seconds to complete the test.

Answer [   ]

SAMPLE DOTS CONCENTRATION TEST 31

Place a diagonal line across each box that contains 4 dots only. You have 30 seconds to complete the test.

Answer [   ]

SAMPLE DOTS CONCENTRATION TEST 32

Place a diagonal line across each box that contains 4 dots only. You have 30 seconds to complete the test.

Answer

SAMPLE DOTS CONCENTRATION TEST 33

Place a diagonal line across each box that contains 4 dots only. You have 30 seconds to complete the test.

Answer [   ]

SAMPLE DOTS CONCENTRATION TEST 34

Place a diagonal line across each box that contains 4 dots only. You have 30 seconds to complete the test.

Answer [   ]

SAMPLE DOTS CONCENTRATION TEST 35

Place a diagonal line across each box that contains 4 dots only. You have 30 seconds to complete the test.

Answer

SAMPLE DOTS CONCENTRATION TEST 36

Place a diagonal line across each box that contains 4 dots only. You have 30 seconds to complete the test.

Answer

SAMPLE DOTS CONCENTRATION TEST 37

Place a diagonal line across each box that contains 4 dots only. You have 30 seconds to complete the test.

Answer [   ]

SAMPLE DOTS CONCENTRATION TEST 38

Place a diagonal line across each box that contains 4 dots only. You have 30 seconds to complete the test.

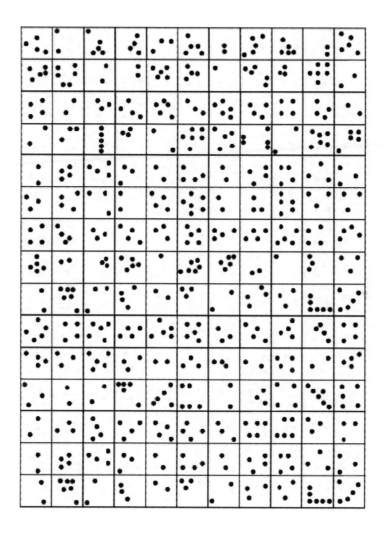

Answer [   ]

SAMPLE DOTS CONCENTRATION TEST 39

Place a diagonal line across each box that contains 4 dots only. You have 30 seconds to complete the test.

Answer

SAMPLE DOTS CONCENTRATION TEST 40

Place a diagonal line across each box that contains 4 dots only. You have 30 seconds to complete the test.

Answer

SAMPLE DOTS CONCENTRATION TEST 41

Place a diagonal line across each box that contains 4 dots only. You have 30 seconds to complete the test.

Answer [   ]

SAMPLE DOTS CONCENTRATION TEST 42

Place a diagonal line across each box that contains 4 dots only. You have 30 seconds to complete the test.

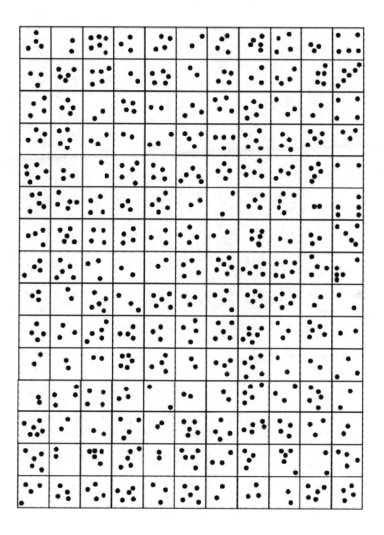

Answer

SAMPLE DOTS CONCENTRATION TEST 43

Place a diagonal line across each box that contains 4 dots only. You have 30 seconds to complete the test.

Answer

SAMPLE DOTS CONCENTRATION TEST 44

Place a diagonal line across each box that contains 4 dots only. You have 30 seconds to complete the test.

Answer

SAMPLE DOTS CONCENTRATION TEST 45

Place a diagonal line across each box that contains 4 dots only. You have 30 seconds to complete the test.

Answer [ ]

SAMPLE DOTS CONCENTRATION TEST 46

Place a diagonal line across each box that contains 4 dots only. You have 30
seconds to complete the test.

Answer

SAMPLE DOTS CONCENTRATION TEST 47

Place a diagonal line across each box that contains 4 dots only. You have 30
seconds to complete the test.

Answer [   ]

SAMPLE DOTS CONCENTRATION TEST 48

Place a diagonal line across each box that contains 4 dots only. You have 30 seconds to complete the test.

Answer

SAMPLE DOTS CONCENTRATION TEST 49

Place a diagonal line across each box that contains 4 dots only. You have 30 seconds to complete the test.

Answer

SAMPLE DOTS CONCENTRATION TESTS 50

Place a diagonal line across each box that contains 4 dots only. You have 30 seconds to complete the test.

Answer

ANSWERS TO DOTS CONCENTRATION TESTS 1 TO 50

1. 20		**26.** 51	
2. 65		**27.** 20	
3. 14		**28.** 37	
4. 44		**29.** 50	
5. 37		**30.** 51	
6. 44		**31.** 46	
7. 33		**32.** 48	
8. 55		**33.** 47	
9. 44		**34.** 44	
10. 44		**35.** 43	
11. 46		**36.** 44	
12. 43		**37.** 38	
13. 38		**39.** 44	
14. 46		**40.** 44	
15. 48		**41.** 48	
16. 44		**42.** 45	
17. 51		**43.** 43	
18. 41		**44.** 41	
19. 43		**45.** 50	
20. 43		**46.** 46	
21. 41		**47.** 41	
22. 42		**48.** 44	
23. 45		**49.** 50	
24. 48		**50.** 42	
25. 55			

CHAPTER SIX
TRAIN DRIVER OBSERVATIONAL ABILITY TEST (OAT)

Becoming a Train Driver requires a person to demonstrate high levels of attention to detail. It is a crucial aspect for any trainee driver to acknowledge this and understand that, to pass the selection process, you must be able to demonstrate these attention skills through a series of tests.

The Train Driver Observational Ability Test (OAT) provides practice and preparation to help improve a person's sustained attention. Your attention will be assessed by engaging with everyday items; whether that be telephone directories or looking for key symbols amongst huge amounts of data.

This test is essential for any aspiring Train Driver. The test is used to determine a person's concentration skills and attention to detail, thus they can gain an overview of the expectations and requirements for proceeding further in the Train Driver profession.

For this test, you will be required to search for fictional phone directories and relevant symbols. You will be given an area code to find which needs to match a particular symbol. Searching the data, you must count how many items have both that symbol and area code. For example, if you are asked to find all the bars with the area code (01947); you must only count the items with the symbol for bars and that area code.

The test is designed to measure levels of concentration, attentiveness and quickness. These sorts of tests are designed to provide a huge amount of information in order to distract you from the actual task. It is important to keep focus, understand what is being asked, and answer the question with precision and efficiency.

For the following questions in this chapter, you have 30 seconds per question.

QUESTION 1

Find all of the bars with the area code (01947)

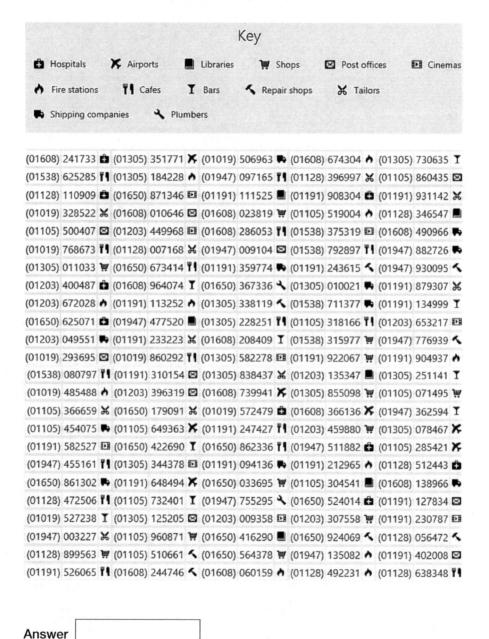

Answer

QUESTION 2

Find all of the plumbers with the area code (01362)

Key

✚ Hospitals	✈ Airports	▦ Libraries	🛒 Shops	✉ Post offices	▣ Cinemas
🔥 Fire stations	🍴 Cafes	🍸 Bars	⚒ Repair shops	✂ Tailors	
🚚 Shipping companies	🔧 Plumbers				

(01764) 239633 🔧 (01362) 966687 🚚 (01916) 110316 🔧 (01865) 833776 ✚ (01362) 512193 🛒
(01294) 430650 ✈ (01294) 686282 ✂ (01362) 235335 🍴 (01879) 848735 🔧 (01865) 111028 🔥
(01916) 415008 ✚ (01777) 774569 🔧 (01916) 842063 🔧 (01294) 399229 ✂ (01879) 188939 ▦
(01916) 905506 🔧 (01610) 791405 🍴 (01294) 842426 🛒 (01359) 150894 🚚 (01879) 936207 ✂
(01411) 192702 ✉ (01865) 032885 🔧 (01610) 332875 🔥 (01764) 137278 ▣ (01359) 976940 🔧
(01916) 444531 ✂ (01879) 252365 🚚 (01865) 910921 🔥 (01777) 774958 🍴 (01359) 051766 ✂
(01294) 168313 🛒 (01865) 512266 🔥 (01916) 442668 ✚ (01411) 191317 ✂ (01359) 202712 🍸
(01294) 287109 ✚ (01362) 127785 🛒 (01764) 906538 🔧 (01294) 834667 ▦ (01916) 128892 🍸
(01916) 750762 🚚 (01916) 104420 ✈ (01865) 435393 🍸 (01610) 777304 ✈ (01879) 102277 🚚
(01879) 807062 ✉ (01764) 549051 🍸 (01610) 532435 🔧 (01865) 332995 🚚 (01916) 356345 ▦
(01294) 337247 🔧 (01777) 938924 🚚 (01610) 570284 🛒 (01879) 351073 🍸 (01362) 162429 ▣
(01777) 067561 🔧 (01362) 804123 🍸 (01879) 014169 🍴 (01359) 139089 ✂ (01916) 196636 ✉
(01879) 516465 🍴 (01610) 566638 🔧 (01362) 209496 🔥 (01411) 604498 🔥 (01294) 662097 ▣
(01777) 895864 🚚 (01764) 729988 🔧 (01359) 465583 🔥 (01359) 655875 🔥 (01294) 040042 🔧
(01610) 813548 🛒 (01879) 767593 🔧 (01777) 795881 🔧 (01359) 818049 ▦ (01916) 647126 ✈
(01916) 678666 🚚 (01879) 441343 🍸 (01879) 112354 🔥 (01411) 061459 🔥 (01879) 190318 ✂
(01865) 794846 ▦ (01411) 163554 🔧 (01764) 443582 🍴 (01362) 975727 🔧 (01879) 728689 🛒
(01865) 345141 🛒 (01362) 630057 ✉ (01865) 091197 🔥 (01359) 782471 ✉ (01764) 480505 🚚
(01764) 127061 🛒 (01294) 001747 🍴 (01879) 388711 ✈ (01610) 303416 ▣ (01916) 674985 ▦
(01610) 255452 🔧 (01777) 177421 🛒 (01764) 460730 🛒 (01359) 691744 🔧 (01764) 362377 🍴
(01777) 677520 ✈ (01865) 666623 ▦ (01362) 658169 🔥 (01764) 218323 🚚 (01865) 921346 ✉
(01777) 324258 🔧 (01610) 441014 ✈ (01359) 629910 ✉ (01777) 066769 🔧 (01294) 669730 ✚
(01777) 513478 ✉ (01879) 347560 ✈ (01294) 008964 🛒 (01879) 448008 🍸 (01359) 378665 🍸
(01865) 897540 🔧 (01359) 191426 🛒 (01777) 437672 🛒 (01865) 772225 🚚 (01879) 198553 🍸

Answer [ ]

QUESTION 3

Find all of the cafes with the area code (01917)

(01497) 849189 🏥 (01762) 890217 ✉ (01122) 110525 ◼ (01508) 829804 🔥 (01497) 473515 🍴
(01475) 548756 ✈ (01917) 945288 🔥 (01246) 581782 🔧 (01508) 889953 ⊥ (01951) 892007 ⊥
(01972) 311189 🎞 (01951) 532280 🔧 (01508) 120905 🎞 (01257) 769388 🍴 (01917) 235406 ✉
(01246) 560703 🔧 (01475) 247223 🏥 (01972) 458873 🛒 (01972) 344506 ✉ (01951) 668522 🚢
(01257) 544161 ✈ (01951) 069950 🚢 (01497) 594397 🛒 (01972) 758940 🔧 (01917) 938445 ✉
(01246) 342373 ✂ (01122) 676514 ⊥ (01122) 604282 🍴 (01475) 200368 🔧 (01508) 592220 ✉
(01246) 519155 🍴 (01917) 471627 ✈ (01951) 491713 ◼ (01246) 718998 ⊥ (01972) 247678 🔧
(01917) 876378 🍴 (01497) 577847 🔧 (01257) 197755 🚢 (01972) 546172 ⊥ (01972) 892019 🍴
(01508) 934166 ⊥ (01257) 188735 🔧 (01951) 273298 🔧 (01917) 595464 🔧 (01508) 986853 ◼
(01972) 875725 ✉ (01122) 425304 ◼ (01122) 564540 ✉ (01257) 657991 ◼ (01122) 414638 🎞
(01972) 610341 🛒 (01497) 014945 🛒 (01762) 948317 🔧 (01257) 592289 🛒 (01475) 815967 🏥
(01972) 740110 ✈ (01951) 308068 🏥 (01475) 417235 🍴 (01917) 334413 🍴 (01122) 567819 🔧
(01972) 921437 ◼ (01257) 120195 🚢 (01257) 490648 🔧 (01917) 365809 🔥 (01475) 162198 ⊥
(01972) 449099 🍴 (01972) 439554 🔥 (01497) 258274 ✈ (01497) 930221 ✈ (01246) 745977 ◼
(01497) 640222 ✉ (01246) 352058 🔧 (01122) 419762 🔧 (01246) 929724 ◼ (01972) 728000 🚢
(01917) 600825 🎞 (01475) 207453 ⊥ (01122) 166790 🔧 (01257) 056368 ✉ (01475) 752280 🔥
(01246) 803348 🚢 (01762) 096534 🔧 (01762) 767479 🎞 (01508) 597146 ⊥ (01257) 264592 ✂
(01497) 215954 🍴 (01497) 674216 🏥 (01122) 509167 🔥 (01497) 442862 ◼ (01917) 543755 ✈
(01951) 477108 ⊥ (01475) 307095 🔧 (01246) 970499 ◼ (01475) 018751 🔧 (01508) 028953 ✂
(01475) 104772 ✉ (01972) 776135 🍴 (01508) 464929 ✈ (01257) 411835 🚢 (01951) 777505 ◼
(01475) 292579 🛒 (01951) 939947 🔥 (01246) 892152 ✉ (01972) 401274 ✉ (01951) 289203 🚢
(01475) 645105 🔥 (01917) 811962 🔧 (01122) 583827 🍴 (01762) 556756 🎞 (01257) 071987 🍴
(01508) 997103 ✂ (01246) 497806 🔧 (01762) 330222 🍴 (01257) 983973 🔥 (01951) 167478 🔧
(01122) 234081 🍴 (01246) 364527 🎞 (01762) 277927 ✂ (01972) 680922 ✉ (01762) 059172 🎞

Answer [   ]

QUESTION 4

Find all of the tailors with the area code (01887)

Key

⊕ Hospitals	✈ Airports	📖 Libraries	🛒 Shops	✉ Post offices	📺 Cinemas
🔥 Fire stations	🍴 Cafes	🍸 Bars	✂ Repair shops	✂ Tailors	
🚢 Shipping companies	🔧 Plumbers				

(01057) 040637 🍴 (01926) 070081 🛒 (01142) 398726 🚢 (01926) 137949 🔥 (01535) 416284 📺
(01144) 047838 📺 (01694) 514966 ⊕ (01966) 524228 ⊕ (01275) 298184 ⊕ (01142) 203392 ✈
(01275) 591078 🔥 (01887) 077583 ✂ (01142) 988561 ✈ (01144) 488639 📺 (01057) 519558 ✂
(01887) 523139 🛒 (01288) 945321 🔧 (01694) 360404 🍸 (01926) 574227 📖 (01535) 273467 🍴
(01887) 741592 ⊕ (01694) 932906 🍴 (01535) 605255 ✂ (01275) 265805 📖 (01142) 575450 🚢
(01142) 236216 ✂ (01142) 752906 🍸 (01887) 145924 🍴 (01144) 909828 🛒 (01144) 616119 ✂
(01535) 562136 🍴 (01887) 400497 🔥 (01887) 202381 🍸 (01535) 432360 📖 (01926) 829119 ✈
(01966) 715604 ⊕ (01887) 436538 🔧 (01275) 959842 🔥 (01535) 483979 🔧 (01535) 289803 🔧
(01142) 052541 ✉ (01926) 592728 ✂ (01887) 403319 ✉ (01694) 064077 🛒 (01142) 463141 📺
(01275) 402908 🚢 (01275) 214803 🍴 (01694) 799647 📺 (01694) 050279 📖 (01966) 503123 📖
(01926) 746781 ✈ (01926) 843129 🍴 (01275) 305461 🔧 (01144) 717968 🔧 (01275) 691216 🍴
(01275) 093721 🛒 (01288) 139692 📖 (01142) 358707 🛒 (01142) 870473 ✂ (01144) 670000 ✂
(01057) 709553 🍴 (01887) 111657 📺 (01887) 733173 🍴 (01144) 983247 ⊕ (01275) 988382 🍸
(01288) 048305 ✉ (01057) 554789 📺 (01535) 807212 🔥 (01142) 551007 🍸 (01057) 405393 🔧
(01926) 853626 📖 (01144) 090414 🔥 (01535) 036461 🔥 (01887) 923379 📖 (01926) 569660 🛒
(01288) 915875 ✂ (01694) 553815 📖 (01142) 063113 ✉ (01142) 093486 🛒 (01926) 738734 ✂
(01535) 689512 🔧 (01275) 824220 🛒 (01694) 217898 ✈ (01057) 854190 🔧 (01142) 283640 ⊕
(01966) 248473 🍴 (01144) 846544 🍴 (01966) 714938 ✂ (01057) 873628 🚢 (01887) 163833 🛒
(01926) 775148 🍸 (01144) 229688 📖 (01144) 979010 🍴 (01887) 743542 🛒 (01966) 269200 📖
(01966) 270905 ✈ (01887) 690206 ✉ (01057) 092772 🍸 (01057) 225300 🔧 (01926) 372883 🔥
(01926) 844866 ✉ (01142) 286285 🚢 (01142) 844109 ✂ (01142) 001946 📺 (01144) 322642 🔥
(01694) 483342 🔧 (01288) 800048 ✈ (01966) 879737 ⊕ (01288) 988672 ✈ (01966) 301677 📺
(01142) 131436 🛒 (01966) 943104 ✂ (01057) 327639 🍸 (01926) 370025 🍸 (01288) 979304 ✂

Answer [   ]

QUESTION 5

Find all of the hospitals with the area code (01983)

	Key				
🏥 Hospitals	✈ Airports	📖 Libraries	🛒 Shops	✉ Post offices	🎞 Cinemas
🔥 Fire stations	🍴 Cafes	⌶ Bars	🔧 Repair shops	✂ Tailors	
🚢 Shipping companies	🔧 Plumbers				

(01983) 531007 🏥 (01659) 023255 🏥 (01862) 691881 🔧 (01964) 077081 ✉ (01964) 566236 🏥
(01735) 806729 🔧 (01659) 999075 ■ (01231) 753170 ✈ (01087) 414782 🎞 (01852) 092499 🏥
(01830) 354392 🔧 (01087) 935038 ⌶ (01231) 725875 ■ (01199) 511629 🏥 (01852) 798485 🍴
(01659) 209970 🔥 (01964) 844670 🍴 (01087) 497741 🏥 (01852) 898628 ✉ (01862) 601403 🚢
(01830) 942835 🚢 (01087) 383029 ✉ (01862) 378617 🔥 (01830) 568733 ■ (01964) 155893 ✈
(01659) 563124 🏥 (01231) 938749 ✈ (01983) 461120 🔧 (01983) 920418 ■ (01852) 312354 ✂
(01199) 722632 ✈ (01199) 318066 🔥 (01199) 086162 🔧 (01964) 042345 🏥 (01964) 423938 🔧
(01830) 200339 🔥 (01659) 987205 ✉ (01735) 642101 🔧 (01735) 277814 ✉ (01231) 255231 🔥
(01659) 569376 ✈ (01830) 882056 ■ (01231) 200847 ■ (01231) 388472 ✉ (01231) 192646 ✈
(01735) 090890 🚢 (01087) 122007 ✂ (01199) 069056 🚢 (01199) 414836 ■ (01964) 136442 ■
(01964) 469045 🎞 (01852) 916766 ⌶ (01659) 775830 🎞 (01087) 304251 ✂ (01231) 033096 🔥
(01087) 620842 ■ (01659) 462557 🏥 (01735) 691743 🎞 (01735) 172599 🏥 (01087) 017250 🛒
(01659) 996026 ✂ (01964) 930486 🚢 (01231) 476818 ■ (01983) 487310 ⌶ (01199) 979485 🔧
(01852) 393910 ✉ (01964) 008423 ✂ (01862) 198258 ⌶ (01830) 002058 🚢 (01862) 567982 🔧
(01862) 118203 🔧 (01862) 977878 🏥 (01199) 645659 🔧 (01735) 023472 ⌶ (01735) 399317 ■
(01231) 449324 🚢 (01862) 684362 ✉ (01862) 510565 🔥 (01964) 189181 ⌶ (01862) 029218 🎞
(01231) 460995 ✈ (01231) 656368 🔥 (01199) 889256 🍴 (01964) 447342 🔥 (01862) 095663 🔧
(01231) 457499 ⌶ (01862) 981464 🔧 (01087) 382241 🏥 (01852) 508290 🔧 (01830) 401436 🔧
(01199) 953532 ■ (01852) 415937 ✈ (01983) 631030 ✉ (01087) 840312 🛒 (01862) 695597 🔧
(01862) 362717 ✂ (01231) 072794 ✉ (01852) 429249 ⌶ (01983) 311828 🔧 (01964) 142454 ✈
(01830) 629112 🎞 (01830) 012149 ⌶ (01087) 734209 ✂ (01087) 317509 🔥 (01199) 922286 🍴
(01087) 237046 ✉ (01087) 344774 🔥 (01231) 744794 🛒 (01830) 532830 🔥 (01087) 180272 🔧
(01735) 211103 ■ (01659) 863265 🚢 (01983) 309535 🏥 (01830) 037144 ■ (01830) 798886 ✉
(01862) 064992 🔥 (01087) 610014 ⌶ (01964) 631568 🍴 (01862) 183130 ⌶ (01852) 114457 🔧

Answer [   ]

QUESTION 6

Find all of the fire stations with the area code (01814)

Key

🏥 Hospitals	✈ Airports	📖 Libraries	🛒 Shops	✉ Post offices	🎬 Cinemas
🔥 Fire stations	🍴 Cafes	🍸 Bars	🔧 Repair shops	✂ Tailors	
🚢 Shipping companies	🔧 Plumbers			

(01982) 867725 ✉ (01757) 557959 🍴 (01977) 109544 🛒 (01083) 629469 🍴 (01066) 515597 🛒
(01910) 690890 🍸 (01757) 868588 🏥 (01066) 097888 🍴 (01910) 290338 📖 (01814) 623704 ✂
(01083) 645620 ✈ (01066) 351315 🍴 (01757) 209321 🍸 (01814) 072745 🏥 (01814) 230071 🔧
(01982) 449585 🍴 (01424) 037342 🍴 (01814) 707490 🔥 (01083) 784235 📖 (01860) 376579 🍴
(01424) 480870 🔥 (01499) 483418 🏥 (01910) 739074 🔧 (01977) 993609 🎬 (01499) 021761 🚢
(01860) 638818 📖 (01066) 559078 🚢 (01066) 229519 ✉ (01757) 642417 🔧 (01910) 338863 🔥
(01757) 042680 ✂ (01066) 507994 🎬 (01757) 939551 ✈ (01860) 640527 🏥 (01860) 174685 ✈
(01982) 601123 ✈ (01814) 004051 🍴 (01977) 726148 🚢 (01066) 157108 🎬 (01424) 307727 🚢
(01499) 083853 🛒 (01424) 317349 🍴 (01814) 233009 🔥 (01977) 059370 🍸 (01083) 272418 🔥
(01910) 854579 🔧 (01424) 501663 🔧 (01977) 776970 ✉ (01814) 335222 ✉ (01083) 278975 🛒
(01083) 051614 🔧 (01977) 677385 🛒 (01083) 175133 🔥 (01424) 020906 🔧 (01499) 858221 🍴
(01424) 082609 🔧 (01757) 083542 📖 (01860) 399246 🎬 (01860) 921375 ✉ (01083) 247859 🍴
(01910) 220258 🛒 (01910) 681984 ✂ (01982) 208196 ✈ (01757) 437388 🍸 (01814) 029520 🏥
(01499) 774316 🔧 (01910) 623173 🎬 (01424) 062374 ✂ (01977) 540770 🍴 (01814) 927748 🎬
(01860) 963935 🏥 (01910) 461565 🛒 (01066) 752789 🎬 (01977) 561998 📖 (01066) 553647 🔧
(01814) 412816 🏥 (01083) 602444 🛒 (01977) 104103 🎬 (01814) 465861 🔧 (01977) 214378 🔧
(01977) 725473 ✉ (01424) 651394 ✂ (01499) 790127 🔧 (01757) 292734 🍸 (01982) 217366 🔧
(01757) 673883 🔧 (01083) 837733 🔥 (01757) 494909 🍴 (01814) 999260 🎬 (01066) 591095 ✉
(01499) 389866 ✉ (01860) 561129 🛒 (01982) 887348 🏥 (01083) 677765 🔧 (01757) 277007 🎬
(01424) 813835 🍸 (01860) 212532 🔧 (01083) 989195 🔥 (01066) 578807 🛒 (01066) 576388 ✂
(01066) 044113 🍴 (01083) 267130 🚢 (01814) 670572 🎬 (01910) 766261 🔥 (01860) 510536 ✈

Answer

[   ]

QUESTION 7

Find all of the libraries with the area code (01734)

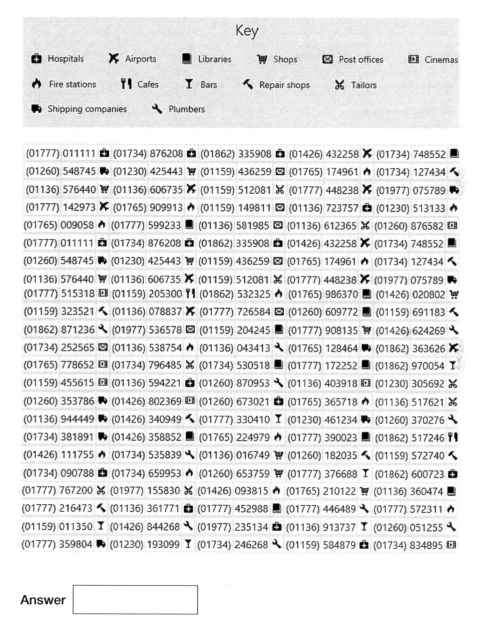

Key

Hospitals   Airports   Libraries   Shops   Post offices   Cinemas

Fire stations   Cafes   Bars   Repair shops   Tailors

Shipping companies   Plumbers

(01777) 011111 ✚ (01734) 876208 ✚ (01862) 335908 ✚ (01426) 432258 ✈ (01734) 748552 ■
(01260) 548745 🚢 (01230) 425443 🛒 (01159) 436259 ✉ (01765) 174961 ♨ (01734) 127434 🔧
(01136) 576440 🛒 (01136) 606735 ✈ (01159) 512081 ✂ (01777) 448238 ✈ (01977) 075789 🚢
(01777) 142973 ✈ (01765) 909913 ♨ (01159) 149811 ✉ (01136) 723757 ✚ (01230) 513133 ♨
(01765) 009058 ♨ (01777) 599233 ■ (01136) 581985 ✉ (01136) 612365 ✂ (01260) 876582 🎬
(01777) 011111 ✚ (01734) 876208 ✚ (01862) 335908 ✚ (01426) 432258 ✈ (01734) 748552 ■
(01260) 548745 🚢 (01230) 425443 🛒 (01159) 436259 ✉ (01765) 174961 ♨ (01734) 127434 🔧
(01136) 576440 🛒 (01136) 606735 ✈ (01159) 512081 ✂ (01777) 448238 ✈ (01977) 075789 🚢
(01777) 515318 🎬 (01159) 205300 🍴 (01862) 532325 ♨ (01765) 986370 ■ (01426) 020802 🛒
(01159) 323521 🔧 (01136) 078837 ✈ (01777) 726584 ✉ (01260) 609772 ■ (01159) 691183 🔧
(01862) 871236 🔧 (01977) 536578 ✉ (01159) 204245 ■ (01777) 908135 🛒 (01426) 624269 🔧
(01734) 252565 ✉ (01136) 538754 ♨ (01136) 043413 🔧 (01765) 128464 🚢 (01862) 363626 ✈
(01765) 778652 🎬 (01734) 796485 ✂ (01734) 530518 ■ (01777) 172252 ■ (01862) 970054 🍸
(01159) 455615 🎬 (01136) 594221 ✚ (01260) 870953 🔧 (01136) 403918 🎬 (01230) 305692 ✂
(01260) 353786 🚢 (01426) 802369 🎬 (01260) 673021 ✚ (01765) 365718 ♨ (01136) 517621 ✂
(01136) 944449 🚢 (01426) 340949 🔧 (01777) 330410 🍸 (01230) 461234 🚢 (01260) 370276 🔧
(01734) 381891 🚢 (01426) 358852 ■ (01765) 224979 ♨ (01777) 390023 ■ (01862) 517246 🍴
(01426) 111755 ♨ (01734) 535839 🔧 (01136) 016749 🛒 (01260) 182035 🔧 (01159) 572740 🔧
(01734) 090788 ✚ (01734) 659953 ♨ (01260) 653759 🛒 (01777) 376688 🍸 (01862) 600723 ✚
(01777) 767200 ✂ (01977) 155830 ✂ (01426) 093815 ♨ (01765) 210122 🛒 (01136) 360474 ■
(01777) 216473 🔧 (01136) 361771 ✚ (01777) 452988 ■ (01777) 446489 🔧 (01777) 572311 ♨
(01159) 011350 🍸 (01426) 844268 🔧 (01977) 235134 ✚ (01136) 913737 🍸 (01260) 051255 🔧
(01777) 359804 🚢 (01230) 193099 🍸 (01734) 246268 🔧 (01159) 584879 ✚ (01734) 834895 🎬

Answer [   ]

QUESTION 8

Find all of the bars with the area code (01103)

Key

✚ Hospitals	✈ Airports	■ Libraries	🛒 Shops	✉ Post offices	🎞 Cinemas
🔥 Fire stations	🍴 Cafes	Ⲓ Bars	⚓ Repair shops	✂ Tailors	
🚢 Shipping companies	🔧 Plumbers				

(01538) 251738 ✚ (01806) 848563 ✉ (01538) 366642 🎞 (01103) 857004 🍴 (01879) 822364 Ⲓ
(01948) 460818 ■ (01063) 379591 ■ (01806) 764782 Ⲓ (01363) 875020 Ⲓ (01138) 086559 🎞
(01806) 677664 🛒 (01900) 887698 Ⲓ (01063) 562299 ■ (01538) 824731 ⚓ (01138) 573088 ✂
(01948) 688310 Ⲓ (01538) 928754 ✈ (01138) 152872 Ⲓ (01103) 012600 ■ (01063) 311389 ✈
(01103) 337745 Ⲓ (01900) 621120 🔥 (01363) 681294 🛒 (01363) 929047 ⚓ (01063) 363429 Ⲓ
(01363) 299423 🎞 (01879) 531166 🚢 (01948) 497515 ■ (01076) 120595 🔧 (01063) 050457 Ⲓ
(01879) 234080 ⚓ (01806) 683695 🔥 (01879) 924820 🔧 (01806) 373417 ⚓ (01538) 393124 🔥
(01138) 024875 ⚓ (01900) 764056 🔧 (01900) 258822 ✂ (01900) 465631 🛒 (01076) 471949 🚢
(01363) 628983 🎞 (01806) 016163 ■ (01806) 118569 🔥 (01806) 461323 ■ (01879) 151433 ⚓
(01063) 660453 ■ (01063) 230861 ✂ (01538) 738605 ✉ (01948) 886383 Ⲓ (01138) 232303 🚢
(01948) 090535 🍴 (01103) 318854 ✈ (01900) 328621 ✉ (01879) 259823 🛒 (01138) 766201 ✈
(01879) 108748 ✉ (01063) 090729 Ⲓ (01076) 069419 ⚓ (01948) 049357 🎞 (01076) 515393 ✉
(01063) 643750 ⚓ (01076) 631447 🔥 (01879) 597065 🚢 (01076) 817775 🎞 (01879) 522253 ⚓
(01879) 357708 🔥 (01948) 927148 🔧 (01538) 946158 ✂ (01806) 479256 ✈ (01900) 377577 🔥
(01948) 188626 Ⲓ (01900) 170693 Ⲓ (01063) 079165 Ⲓ (01806) 016352 🛒 (01948) 771939 ✂
(01879) 659248 ⚓ (01879) 374935 🔥 (01138) 478567 🔧 (01879) 872398 🎞 (01103) 980463 🔧
(01363) 102195 🛒 (01806) 276133 ⚓ (01063) 537540 ⚓ (01063) 889280 ■ (01948) 755454 🍴
(01138) 306076 ✂ (01063) 401148 🛒 (01076) 953815 ✉ (01538) 720136 ✉ (01900) 227747 🎞
(01948) 688310 Ⲓ (01538) 928754 ✈ (01138) 152872 Ⲓ (01103) 012600 ■ (01063) 311389 ✈
(01103) 337745 Ⲓ (01900) 621120 🔥 (01363) 681294 🛒 (01363) 929047 ⚓ (01063) 363429 Ⲓ

Answer [   ]

QUESTION 9

Find all of the shops with the area code (01923)

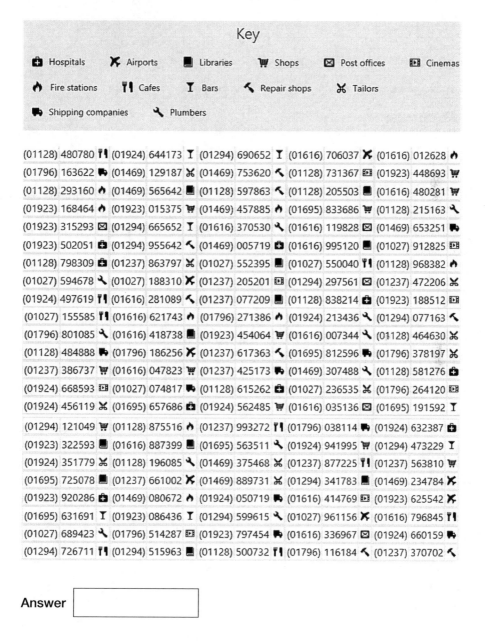

Key

Hospitals   Airports   Libraries   Shops   Post offices   Cinemas

Fire stations   Cafes   Bars   Repair shops   Tailors

Shipping companies   Plumbers

(01128) 480780 ¶ (01924) 644173 I (01294) 690652 I (01616) 706037 ✘ (01616) 012628 ♦
(01796) 163622 ➠ (01469) 129187 ✄ (01469) 753620 ⬧ (01128) 731367 ▦ (01923) 448693 ♚
(01128) 293160 ♦ (01469) 565642 ■ (01128) 597863 ⬧ (01128) 205503 ■ (01616) 480281 ♚
(01923) 168464 ♦ (01923) 015375 ♚ (01469) 457885 ♦ (01695) 833686 ♚ (01128) 215163 ⚒
(01923) 315293 ✉ (01294) 665652 I (01616) 370530 ⚒ (01616) 119828 ✉ (01469) 653251 ➠
(01923) 502051 ✚ (01294) 955642 ⬧ (01469) 005719 ✚ (01616) 995120 ■ (01027) 912825 ▦
(01128) 798309 ✚ (01237) 863797 ✄ (01027) 552395 ■ (01027) 550040 ¶ (01128) 968382 ♦
(01027) 594678 ⚒ (01027) 188310 ✘ (01237) 205201 ▦ (01294) 297561 ✉ (01237) 472206 ✄
(01924) 497619 ¶ (01616) 281089 ⬧ (01237) 077209 ■ (01128) 838214 ✚ (01923) 188512 ▦
(01027) 155585 ¶ (01616) 621743 ♦ (01796) 271386 ♦ (01924) 213436 ⚒ (01294) 077163 ⬧
(01796) 801085 ⚒ (01616) 418738 ■ (01923) 454064 ♚ (01616) 007344 ⚒ (01128) 464630 ✄
(01128) 484888 ➠ (01796) 186256 ✘ (01237) 617363 ⬧ (01695) 812596 ➠ (01796) 378197 ✄
(01237) 386737 ♚ (01616) 047823 ♚ (01237) 425173 ➠ (01469) 307488 ⚒ (01128) 581276 ✚
(01924) 668593 ▦ (01027) 074817 ➠ (01128) 615262 ✚ (01027) 236535 ✄ (01796) 264120 ▦
(01924) 456119 ✄ (01695) 657686 ✚ (01924) 562485 ♚ (01616) 035136 ✉ (01695) 191592 I
(01294) 121049 ♚ (01128) 875516 ♦ (01237) 993272 ¶ (01796) 038114 ➠ (01924) 632387 ✚
(01923) 322593 ■ (01616) 887399 ■ (01695) 563511 ⚒ (01924) 941995 ♚ (01294) 473229 I
(01924) 351779 ✄ (01128) 196085 ⚒ (01469) 375468 ✄ (01237) 877225 ¶ (01237) 563810 ♚
(01695) 725078 ■ (01237) 661002 ✘ (01469) 889731 ✄ (01294) 341783 ■ (01469) 234784 ✘
(01923) 920286 ✚ (01469) 080672 ♦ (01924) 050719 ➠ (01616) 414769 ▦ (01923) 625542 ✘
(01695) 631691 I (01923) 086436 I (01294) 599615 ⚒ (01027) 961156 ✘ (01616) 796845 ¶
(01027) 689423 ⚒ (01796) 514287 ▦ (01923) 797454 ➠ (01616) 336967 ✉ (01924) 660159 ➠
(01294) 726711 ¶ (01294) 515963 ■ (01128) 500732 ¶ (01796) 116184 ⬧ (01237) 370702 ⬧

Answer [   ]

QUESTION 10

Find all of the shipping companies with the area code (01662)

Key

✚ Hospitals	✈ Airports	▥ Libraries	🛒 Shops	✉ Post offices	▦ Cinemas
🔥 Fire stations	🍴 Cafes	🍸 Bars	🔧 Repair shops	✂ Tailors	
🚚 Shipping companies	🔧 Plumbers				

(01479) 880910 ✈ (01211) 879429 ▥ (01999) 937256 ✉ (01591) 660552 🍴 (01802) 442706 🔥
(01987) 038502 🔧 (01808) 712332 ✉ (01591) 035297 ▦ (01802) 074107 ✚ (01987) 287200 🍸
(01808) 601501 🚚 (01987) 878843 ✚ (01662) 019466 🚚 (01005) 550271 🛒 (01802) 169033 ▥
(01999) 193014 ✂ (01479) 819197 ✂ (01211) 536284 🍸 (01591) 714557 🍸 (01808) 140913 🛒
(01808) 686558 ✈ (01987) 643850 🔥 (01005) 463653 🔥 (01662) 088544 ✚ (01005) 089532 🚚
(01802) 198969 ✈ (01808) 281409 ▦ (01808) 888115 🔧 (01187) 240256 🔥 (01005) 323460 ▦
(01802) 613824 🔧 (01808) 121440 ▥ (01808) 730183 🔥 (01662) 287250 🍸 (01999) 750269 ✉
(01999) 802331 🛒 (01187) 565045 ✈ (01662) 803587 🔧 (01808) 405003 🔧 (01999) 955798 ▥
(01187) 078116 🔧 (01802) 287505 ▦ (01187) 676285 ✈ (01479) 617916 🛒 (01187) 789972 ✉
(01479) 340052 ✈ (01802) 235213 🔧 (01187) 327954 🍸 (01999) 763836 🍸 (01808) 275728 ✚
(01999) 322745 ✚ (01999) 658179 ✈ (01591) 976642 🍴 (01187) 140772 🛒 (01802) 802481 🔥
(01479) 332053 ✚ (01999) 773167 🔧 (01591) 043193 ▥ (01211) 452518 ▦ (01005) 376533 🔥
(01808) 336417 ✉ (01802) 410342 🍸 (01211) 899559 ✉ (01479) 462551 🔧 (01999) 503216 🍸
(01662) 539532 ✈ (01211) 167343 🔧 (01479) 476489 ✉ (01005) 065793 ✂ (01662) 598556 ✚
(01808) 665303 🔥 (01187) 112668 🛒 (01591) 610580 ▥ (01187) 654631 🍸 (01187) 215249 🚚
(01211) 509648 🍴 (01662) 247724 🚚 (01479) 544297 🔧 (01591) 935492 🚚 (01808) 807460 ✈
(01211) 348749 ✂ (01211) 226371 ✈ (01999) 406892 🛒 (01211) 923767 🛒 (01479) 282754 🚚
(01662) 527107 🔥 (01591) 264698 🔧 (01662) 160498 🔧 (01211) 743629 🚚 (01802) 387845 🛒
(01802) 102015 ▦ (01808) 841530 ✈ (01211) 731958 ✈ (01479) 315396 🔥 (01802) 620169 ✈
(01211) 882313 🔧 (01591) 360396 🔧 (01187) 410851 🍴 (01662) 837833 ✂ (01802) 211254 🔧

Answer [   ]

QUESTION 11

Find all of the post offices with the area code (01231)

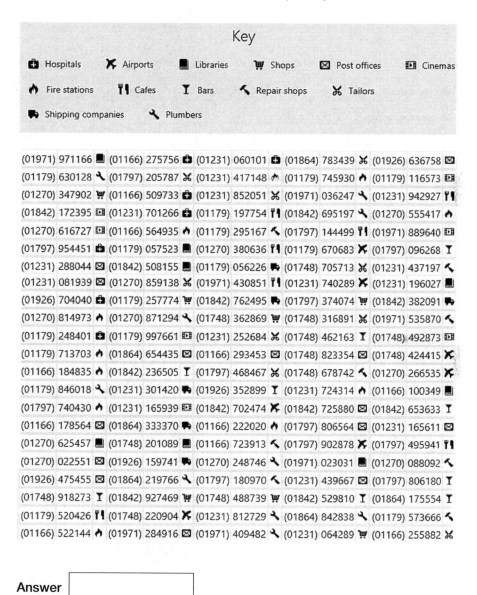

Key

🏥 Hospitals   ✈ Airports   ■ Libraries   🛒 Shops   ✉ Post offices   🎬 Cinemas

🔥 Fire stations   🍴 Cafes   🍸 Bars   🔧 Repair shops   ✂ Tailors

🚚 Shipping companies   🔧 Plumbers

(01971) 971166 ■ (01166) 275756 🏥 (01231) 060101 🏥 (01864) 783439 ✂ (01926) 636758 ✉
(01179) 630128 🔧 (01797) 205787 ✂ (01231) 417148 🔥 (01179) 745930 🔥 (01179) 116573 🎬
(01270) 347902 🛒 (01166) 509733 🏥 (01231) 852051 ✂ (01971) 036247 🔧 (01231) 942927 🍴
(01842) 172395 🎬 (01231) 701266 🏥 (01179) 197754 🍴 (01842) 695197 🔧 (01270) 555417 🔥
(01270) 616727 🎬 (01166) 564935 🔥 (01179) 295167 🔧 (01797) 144499 🍴 (01971) 889640 🎬
(01797) 954451 🏥 (01179) 057523 ■ (01270) 380636 🍴 (01179) 670683 ✂ (01797) 096268 🍸
(01231) 288044 ✉ (01842) 508155 ■ (01179) 056226 🚚 (01748) 705713 ✂ (01231) 437197 🔧
(01231) 081939 ✉ (01270) 859138 ✂ (01971) 430851 🍴 (01231) 740289 ✂ (01231) 196027 ■
(01926) 704040 🏥 (01179) 257774 🛒 (01842) 762495 🚚 (01797) 374074 🛒 (01842) 382091 🚚
(01270) 814973 🔥 (01270) 871294 🔧 (01748) 362869 🛒 (01748) 316891 ✂ (01971) 535870 🔧
(01179) 248401 🏥 (01179) 997661 🎬 (01231) 252684 ✂ (01748) 462163 🍸 (01748) 492873 🎬
(01179) 713703 🔥 (01864) 654435 ✉ (01166) 293453 ✉ (01748) 823354 ✉ (01748) 424415 ✂
(01166) 184835 🔥 (01842) 236505 🍸 (01797) 468467 ✂ (01748) 678742 🔧 (01270) 266535 ✂
(01179) 846018 🔧 (01231) 301420 🚚 (01926) 352899 🍸 (01231) 724314 🔥 (01166) 100349 ■
(01797) 740430 🔥 (01231) 165939 🎬 (01842) 702474 ✂ (01842) 725880 ✉ (01842) 653633 🍸
(01166) 178564 ✉ (01864) 333370 🚚 (01166) 222020 🔥 (01797) 806564 ✉ (01231) 165611 ✉
(01270) 625457 ■ (01748) 201089 ■ (01166) 723913 🔧 (01797) 902878 ✂ (01797) 495941 🍴
(01270) 022551 ✉ (01926) 159741 🚚 (01270) 248746 🔧 (01971) 023031 ■ (01270) 088092 🔧
(01926) 475455 ✉ (01864) 219766 🔧 (01797) 180970 🔧 (01231) 439667 ✉ (01797) 806180 🍸
(01748) 918273 🍸 (01842) 927469 🛒 (01748) 488739 🛒 (01842) 529810 🍸 (01864) 175554 🍸
(01179) 520426 🍴 (01748) 220904 ✂ (01231) 812729 🔧 (01864) 842838 🔧 (01179) 573666 🔧
(01166) 522144 🔥 (01971) 284916 ✉ (01971) 409482 🔧 (01231) 064289 🛒 (01166) 255882 ✂

Answer [ ]

QUESTION 12

Find all of the cinemas with the area code (01451)

Key

🏥 Hospitals	✈ Airports	▪ Libraries	🛒 Shops	✉ Post offices	▣ Cinemas
🔥 Fire stations	🍴 Cafes	Y Bars	✖ Repair shops	✂ Tailors	
🚢 Shipping companies	🔧 Plumbers				

(01612) 524606 ▣ (01573) 424451 ✉ (01612) 083816 🔧 (01499) 959706 🚢 (01573) 045769 🔧
(01762) 480119 🔧 (01612) 720293 🛒 (01583) 616108 ✖ (01583) 163335 🍴 (01575) 100062 🍴
(01473) 092408 ✉ (01451) 717427 ▣ (01440) 520055 🛒 (01451) 166243 🔧 (01451) 194629 🔧
(01473) 464196 🔧 (01451) 868965 🏥 (01516) 272717 Y (01573) 290070 🔧 (01575) 809141 🏥
(01451) 350856 Y (01575) 504436 ▣ (01573) 259299 Y (01440) 494923 ✖ (01575) 305593 🔥
(01499) 183193 ▣ (01762) 586232 Y (01612) 570013 🔧 (01451) 748525 ✖ (01573) 490599 ▣
(01762) 220470 ▣ (01583) 317711 🔧 (01573) 541656 🛒 (01612) 357192 🛒 (01451) 919948 🚢
(01473) 064144 🍴 (01573) 095682 ▣ (01516) 435181 🛒 (01499) 524384 🏥 (01575) 737080 ✂
(01451) 765283 🔧 (01762) 711182 ▪ (01583) 901825 🔧 (01575) 003202 🔥 (01762) 180633 🍴
(01473) 516545 🔥 (01573) 775747 ▪ (01516) 973292 🛒 (01440) 081177 ✖ (01473) 689095 ✂
(01473) 653592 🏥 (01451) 030352 ✉ (01575) 683728 🛒 (01473) 786902 🔥 (01473) 930940 ✂
(01516) 701591 🍴 (01451) 539790 ▣ (01516) 672645 ✖ (01575) 457278 ▪ (01583) 079298 ✖
(01583) 866016 🔧 (01612) 229664 🍴 (01499) 708688 ▪ (01575) 855880 🛒 (01499) 517691 ✂
(01451) 187933 ▣ (01473) 107133 ✖ (01762) 913652 🔧 (01516) 423232 ✉ (01440) 224031 🍴
(01762) 599984 ✂ (01516) 386338 ▪ (01573) 266596 🔧 (01440) 513515 🔥 (01762) 476434 🔥
(01451) 939950 ✉ (01612) 428827 🔧 (01451) 495115 ✂ (01440) 321910 🔧 (01762) 678448 ✖
(01516) 635896 ✉ (01440) 735963 🔧 (01451) 405250 ▣ (01575) 300263 🏥 (01499) 783562 🔥
(01499) 805695 ✖ (01612) 905317 ▣ (01612) 271299 🚢 (01583) 917135 ▪ (01499) 559817 ✖

Answer [   ]

QUESTION 13

Find all of the post offices with the area code (01010)

	Key	
⊞ Hospitals ✈ Airports ▪ Libraries 🛒 Shops ⊠ Post offices ▤ Cinemas		
♦ Fire stations 🍴 Cafes Ⴈ Bars 🔧 Repair shops ✂ Tailors		
🚢 Shipping companies ⚒ Plumbers		

(01132) 602357 ✈ (01967) 773133 ⚒ (01010) 338206 ⊠ (01624) 648365 🚢 (01667) 285928 ✈
(01373) 182374 ⚒ (01373) 032526 ▤ (01624) 085128 🍴 (01093) 466576 Ⴈ (01017) 898917 ⊠
(01327) 955866 🍴 (01017) 664670 🚢 (01373) 764327 ⚒ (01093) 019502 ✈ (01373) 611177 ♦
(01824) 121665 ⚒ (01132) 665772 ▪ (01624) 406202 ⊞ (01093) 559843 ♦ (01327) 314804 🛒
(01017) 998641 Ⴈ (01667) 342636 🍴 (01093) 165147 ⊞ (01093) 985288 ⚒ (01667) 266926 ♦
(01010) 194339 🍴 (01624) 064875 ✈ (01373) 189393 ⊞ (01624) 444745 ⚒ (01967) 078610 ✂
(01010) 978112 ⊠ (01667) 263901 ▪ (01824) 406466 ▤ (01010) 296588 ✂ (01824) 761374 Ⴈ
(01017) 481258 🍴 (01824) 666043 ✂ (01967) 880085 ⚒ (01967) 164122 ⚒ (01010) 647870 🍴
(01667) 755335 ▤ (01132) 051705 ⊞ (01667) 676037 ✂ (01327) 150302 ▪ (01132) 334505 ✈
(01373) 183023 ✂ (01667) 037931 ▤ (01327) 961637 🍴 (01373) 810946 ⚒ (01010) 839816 ⊠
(01667) 655336 🚢 (01967) 102166 ⊠ (01967) 875440 ✂ (01967) 627120 Ⴈ (01017) 314527 ✈
(01373) 334347 Ⴈ (01824) 029918 ▪ (01373) 477840 ⊠ (01327) 832786 ✈ (01017) 836217 ▪
(01667) 642337 ⚒ (01327) 660810 ▪ (01010) 368097 ▪ (01093) 969967 ⊠ (01017) 724170 ▤
(01093) 337718 ▤ (01017) 278219 ✂ (01010) 340406 ⚒ (01093) 678436 ♦ (01373) 762806 ⚒
(01373) 183023 ✂ (01667) 037931 ▤ (01327) 961637 🍴 (01373) 810946 ⚒ (01010) 839816 ⊠
(01667) 655336 🚢 (01967) 102166 ⊠ (01967) 875440 ✂ (01967) 627120 Ⴈ (01017) 314527 ✈
(01327) 235200 Ⴈ (01373) 473695 ▤ (01010) 083326 ⚒ (01373) 084585 ▪ (01010) 579944 ⊠
(01017) 007287 🚢 (01010) 143897 ⚒ (01624) 881532 ♦ (01824) 613283 ✈ (01132) 594340 ♦
(01373) 557342 ♦ (01667) 225158 🚢 (01017) 096082 🛒 (01624) 232864 Ⴈ (01967) 288998 ✂
(01824) 904474 ✂ (01624) 974681 ✂ (01373) 376667 Ⴈ (01017) 122885 ♦ (01017) 311865 ▤

Answer [   ]

QUESTION 14

Find all of the airports with the area code (01233)

Key

Hospitals	Airports	Libraries	Shops	Post offices	Cinemas
Fire stations	Cafes	Bars	Repair shops	Tailors	
Shipping companies	Plumbers				

(01509) 799196 🛒 (01002) 496246 I (01509) 883208 🛒 (01304) 045030 🍴 (01632) 155984 ✂
(01509) 897614 ← (01636) 792315 ♦ (01304) 814912 ✈ (01167) 796173 🎦 (01309) 189903 ✈
(01233) 794246 🔧 (01984) 284025 🔧 (01167) 556648 📖 (01632) 109230 ✚ (01378) 942591 🛒
(01304) 375908 ← (01509) 730350 I (01304) 389453 ♦ (01167) 193984 🔧 (01632) 239086 🍴
(01002) 185477 📖 (01984) 608793 🚢 (01509) 883004 🛒 (01378) 491695 ✈ (01304) 453860 I
(01984) 843662 🎦 (01378) 682056 ✂ (01233) 454333 ← (01233) 466800 ✈ (01233) 958676 ♦
(01509) 532957 🚢 (01233) 115635 🍴 (01632) 588118 🛒 (01984) 012354 ← (01984) 946148 ✈
(01167) 178335 🍴 (01984) 607097 🛒 (01509) 869199 📖 (01378) 334419 🚢 (01002) 723547 ✈
(01233) 903112 🍴 (01378) 070559 📖 (01304) 396127 ← (01632) 488002 🎦 (01378) 504643 🎦
(01304) 835461 ✈ (01002) 869678 ✂ (01632) 844213 🎦 (01309) 661992 🔧 (01984) 668681 I
(01002) 172054 🛒 (01378) 190257 📖 (01167) 891092 ← (01378) 853419 ✂ (01002) 864926 ←
(01167) 779115 🎦 (01304) 762199 🎦 (01233) 233683 🔧 (01378) 136436 🎦 (01309) 223502 ✂
(01233) 102239 I (01002) 154277 ✈ (01304) 226444 ✚ (01304) 414892 🛒 (01632) 019279 🚢
(01309) 700511 📖 (01632) 582610 🔧 (01378) 205707 🛒 (01632) 321635 🛒 (01632) 793533 ✚
(01309) 931613 ✚ (01984) 163900 ♦ (01002) 574703 ✚ (01002) 399492 ✂ (01636) 145399 ✚
(01304) 089970 🍴 (01509) 215560 ✂ (01233) 815778 ✈ (01984) 363737 ♦ (01378) 852322 ✂
(01378) 001083 ✉ (01233) 231215 🛒 (01233) 404526 🛒 (01378) 152701 🛒 (01167) 170336 🛒
(01309) 691592 I (01233) 471175 📖 (01233) 144533 ✈ (01509) 924306 ✂ (01636) 043672 ✂
(01636) 262724 ✂ (01304) 869792 🍴 (01233) 408339 🛒 (01509) 949676 ✉ (01233) 622263 🎦
(01002) 571725 ← (01002) 563472 ← (01636) 504515 ✉ (01984) 828573 🍴 (01984) 897054 🚢
(01378) 327432 ✈ (01002) 933120 🎦 (01233) 955751 🛒 (01167) 402668 I (01509) 840778 📖
(01636) 674928 🔧 (01636) 118182 ♦ (01304) 085052 🚢 (01233) 484413 ✚ (01002) 002020 ✂
(01309) 388471 ✂ (01636) 232808 🎦 (01984) 022923 ← (01984) 457021 🛒 (01984) 101830 🍴
(01167) 112399 📖 (01984) 655367 ✈ (01167) 380404 ✈ (01002) 256319 ♦ (01509) 372913 🛒

Answer [   ]

QUESTION 15

Find all of the plumbers with the area code (01917)

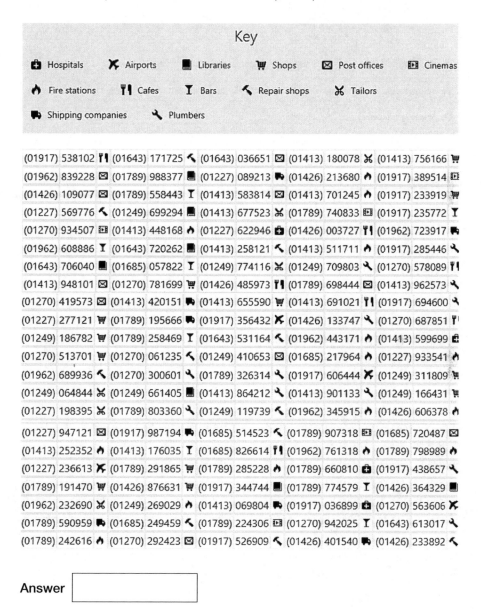

Key

🏥 Hospitals   ✈ Airports   ▪ Libraries   🛒 Shops   ✉ Post offices   🎞 Cinemas

🔥 Fire stations   🍴 Cafes   ⊺ Bars   🔧 Repair shops   ✂ Tailors

🚚 Shipping companies   🔧 Plumbers

(01917) 538102 🍴 (01643) 171725 🔧 (01643) 036651 ✉ (01413) 180078 ✂ (01413) 756166 🛒
(01962) 839228 ✉ (01789) 988377 ▪ (01227) 089213 🚚 (01426) 213680 🔥 (01917) 389514 🎞
(01426) 109077 ✉ (01789) 558443 ⊺ (01413) 583814 ✉ (01413) 701245 🔥 (01917) 233919 🛒
(01227) 569776 🔧 (01249) 699294 ▪ (01413) 677523 ✂ (01789) 740833 🎞 (01917) 235772 ⊺
(01270) 934507 🎞 (01413) 448168 🔥 (01227) 622946 🏥 (01426) 003727 🍴 (01962) 723917 🚚
(01962) 608886 ⊺ (01643) 720262 ▪ (01413) 258121 🔧 (01413) 511711 🔥 (01917) 285446 🔧
(01643) 706040 ▪ (01685) 057822 ⊺ (01249) 774116 ✂ (01249) 709803 🔧 (01270) 578089 🍴
(01413) 948101 ✉ (01270) 781699 🛒 (01426) 485973 🍴 (01789) 698444 ✉ (01413) 962573 🔧
(01270) 419573 ✉ (01413) 420151 🚚 (01413) 655590 🛒 (01413) 691021 🍴 (01917) 694600 🔧
(01227) 277121 🛒 (01789) 195666 🚚 (01917) 356432 ✈ (01426) 133747 🔧 (01270) 687851 🍴
(01249) 186782 🛒 (01789) 258469 ⊺ (01643) 531164 🔧 (01962) 443171 🔥 (01413) 599699 🏥
(01270) 513701 🛒 (01270) 061235 🔧 (01249) 410653 ✉ (01685) 217964 🔥 (01227) 933541 🔥
(01962) 689936 🔧 (01270) 300601 🔧 (01789) 326314 🔧 (01917) 606444 ✈ (01249) 311809 🛒
(01249) 064844 ✂ (01249) 661405 ▪ (01413) 864212 🔧 (01413) 901133 🔧 (01249) 166431 🛒
(01227) 198395 ✂ (01789) 803360 🔧 (01249) 119739 🔧 (01962) 345915 🔥 (01426) 606378 🔥

(01227) 947121 ✉ (01917) 987194 🚚 (01685) 514523 🔧 (01789) 907318 🎞 (01685) 720487 ✉
(01413) 252352 🔥 (01413) 176035 ⊺ (01685) 826614 🍴 (01962) 761318 🔥 (01789) 798989 🔥
(01227) 236613 ✈ (01789) 291865 🛒 (01789) 285228 🔥 (01789) 660810 🏥 (01917) 438657 🔧
(01789) 191470 🛒 (01426) 876631 🛒 (01917) 344744 ▪ (01789) 774579 ⊺ (01426) 364329 ▪
(01962) 232690 ✂ (01249) 269029 🔥 (01413) 069804 🚚 (01917) 036899 🏥 (01270) 563606 ✈
(01789) 590959 🚚 (01685) 249459 🔧 (01789) 224306 🎞 (01270) 942025 ⊺ (01643) 613017 🔧
(01789) 242616 🔥 (01270) 292423 ✉ (01917) 526909 🔧 (01426) 401540 🚚 (01426) 233892 🔧

Answer

QUESTION 16

Find all of the cinemas with the area code (01891)

Key

✚ Hospitals	✈ Airports	▥ Libraries	🛒 Shops	✉ Post offices	▣ Cinemas
♨ Fire stations	🍴 Cafes	⊺ Bars	⚟ Repair shops	✄ Tailors	
🚢 Shipping companies	⚒ Plumbers				

(01605) 450303 ✚ (01302) 959955 ⚒ (01684) 363495 ⊺ (01320) 527604 ✄ (01338) 615373 ▣
(01302) 764508 ✈ (01890) 273324 ✚ (01302) 947481 🛒 (01524) 837929 🍴 (01320) 381296 🚢
(01891) 743538 ⚒ (01338) 903614 ⚒ (01605) 593304 ⊺ (01709) 413048 ▣ (01890) 753768 ▣
(01890) 562271 🛒 (01709) 304122 🛒 (01302) 149234 🛒 (01605) 790388 ▣ (01890) 449151 ▣
(01709) 786272 🛒 (01320) 871664 ✉ (01091) 460389 ⚒ (01091) 488391 ♨ (01709) 604534 ▣
(01302) 866937 ✉ (01709) 304710 🚢 (01684) 587315 🚢 (01338) 660058 ✄ (01890) 521692 ⚟
(01709) 171865 ✄ (01709) 158721 ✚ (01891) 073963 🍴 (01302) 249627 ✄ (01709) 804264 ▣
(01320) 796421 ✉ (01338) 343413 ✚ (01524) 183711 ✚ (01320) 877202 ♨ (01709) 548740 ▣
(01302) 883465 ⚟ (01891) 038509 ✄ (01320) 044797 ⊺ (01891) 131855 ✉ (01890) 234795 ⚟
(01091) 747066 ▣ (01891) 338820 ▣ (01890) 121062 🛒 (01338) 993081 🍴 (01338) 273498 ⊺
(01891) 687482 ♨ (01890) 442070 ✚ (01891) 044146 ✚ (01338) 708506 ✚ (01091) 708384 ▣
(01684) 292605 ⚒ (01320) 032220 ▥ (01709) 050337 ▣ (01684) 442040 ✉ (01091) 240838 ♨
(01338) 042424 🚢 (01091) 880924 ✚ (01524) 663755 ✚ (01091) 373483 ✈ (01091) 382491 ⊺
(01709) 842186 ✈ (01891) 064074 ⚒ (01302) 317113 ⚟ (01091) 183595 🚢 (01605) 127397 ✉
(01091) 400151 ♨ (01338) 368981 🛒 (01524) 958314 ▣ (01709) 553312 ▣ (01320) 747932 ▥
(01302) 983696 ⚒ (01709) 269432 ⊺ (01890) 958375 🚢 (01338) 795224 ♨ (01091) 726241 🛒
(01891) 020171 ⚟ (01338) 315065 🍴 (01890) 753564 ✚ (01709) 707723 ⊺ (01302) 541659 ♨
(01890) 514636 🚢 (01890) 949934 🚢 (01709) 705868 ▥ (01302) 622480 ▥ (01524) 790558 ✚
(01890) 186081 ⚟ (01684) 759368 ♨ (01890) 615716 🚢 (01524) 903992 ✉ (01684) 007908 ⚒
(01890) 355122 ⊺ (01524) 590532 🍴 (01684) 323399 ▥ (01091) 513907 ▣ (01605) 378923 ▥
(01891) 039717 ✈ (01320) 924748 🍴 (01890) 969040 ⊺ (01091) 044872 ⚒ (01302) 588804 ✈

Answer _____

QUESTION 17

Find all of the post offices with the area code (01790)

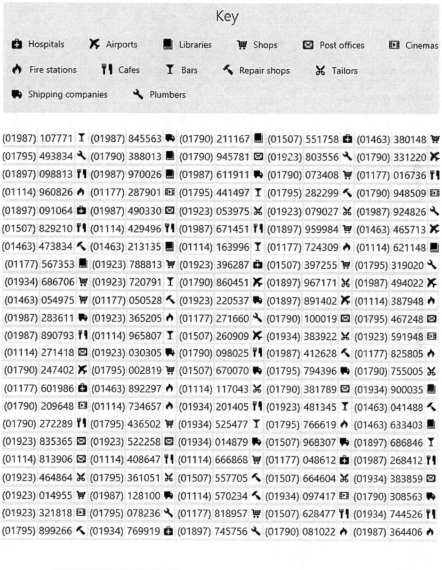

Answer

QUESTION 18

Find all of the repair shops with the area code (01990)

Key

✚ Hospitals	✈ Airports	▇ Libraries	🛒 Shops	✉ Post offices	🎬 Cinemas
🔥 Fire stations	🍴 Cafes	🍸 Bars	◄ Repair shops	✂ Tailors	
🚚 Shipping companies	🔧 Plumbers				

(01517) 475467 🔧 (01943) 206427 ✉ (01340) 128884 🔥 (01517) 312083 ▇ (01634) 083976 🛒
(01990) 603329 🎬 (01817) 744828 🚚 (01634) 599009 ✚ (01634) 467806 ✂ (01435) 844488 ✚
(01925) 517573 ◄ (01634) 654549 ◄ (01634) 584687 🛒 (01925) 095926 🛒 (01990) 744695 ◄
(01764) 570001 🚚 (01817) 342264 ✈ (01990) 385265 🔧 (01817) 963436 ✂ (01817) 519649 🔥
(01663) 443894 ▇ (01435) 462525 🚚 (01663) 526317 🔧 (01764) 174097 ✉ (01925) 627193 ✂
(01943) 293793 🍴 (01817) 911364 ◄ (01817) 898460 ✉ (01990) 792328 🔥 (01634) 942430 🛒
(01943) 813632 🛒 (01925) 125769 🛒 (01943) 854532 🛒 (01435) 941362 🍸 (01925) 766859 🎬
(01634) 138145 🔥 (01663) 168935 ▇ (01943) 756787 ✚ (01943) 836623 ✂ (01990) 315585 ✂
(01943) 676872 🍸 (01990) 074884 ◄ (01340) 521761 🔧 (01990) 368678 🔧 (01764) 099741 🍴
(01517) 872782 🚚 (01634) 031154 ✉ (01943) 106903 ✉ (01663) 274307 ✚ (01925) 433513 🎬
(01435) 455047 ✈ (01990) 954234 🍴 (01435) 711289 🎬 (01943) 551419 ✂ (01943) 190824 🛒
(01925) 107288 ✈ (01340) 236487 ◄ (01990) 776432 ✚ (01764) 920926 🔧 (01943) 045645 🚚
(01925) 581894 🔧 (01817) 299762 🔥 (01634) 208994 ◄ (01943) 226439 🔥 (01943) 628180 ✂
(01990) 432548 🔧 (01663) 660160 🎬 (01764) 251848 🚚 (01517) 577596 🍴 (01990) 527468 ✈
(01663) 968704 🚚 (01817) 834523 ✚ (01663) 007639 ✉ (01943) 417667 🚚 (01817) 244566 🍸
(01925) 177618 🚚 (01634) 018514 🚚 (01764) 482031 🔧 (01340) 079922 🍴 (01340) 909853 ✂
(01663) 613242 🍴 (01943) 581690 ✂ (01435) 790395 🚚 (01663) 600279 ◄ (01764) 534979 ✈
(01435) 192862 🍴 (01925) 671209 🔧 (01340) 199704 🎬 (01990) 982511 🛒 (01764) 505473 🎬
(01663) 546139 🔥 (01925) 309924 🚚 (01817) 845663 ▇ (01943) 035464 ◄ (01340) 159772 ✉
(01764) 811364 ✚ (01517) 987308 ✈ (01817) 857586 ✉ (01435) 128350 ✉ (01764) 537328 ▇
(01990) 444403 ✂ (01435) 275507 ✚ (01925) 232524 ✉ (01435) 344201 🎬 (01340) 220955 ✉
(01943) 088917 ✚ (01925) 243927 ✈ (01634) 276604 🍴 (01990) 141860 🚚 (01943) 571612 🚚

Answer

QUESTION 19

Find all of the shipping companies with the area code (01281)

Key

🏥 Hospitals   ✈ Airports   📕 Libraries   🛒 Shops   ✉ Post offices   🎞 Cinemas

🔥 Fire stations   🍴 Cafes   Ⲁ Bars   🔧 Repair shops   ✂ Tailors

🚚 Shipping companies   🔧 Plumbers

(01463) 271481 ✉ (01463) 927821 Ⲁ (01403) 257342 📕 (01307) 158519 🛒 (01281) 325212 🚚
(01281) 519439 🍴 (01818) 896885 🏥 (01818) 319163 📕 (01281) 226810 📕 (01664) 393988 🚚
(01307) 650001 🔧 (01635) 813739 🏥 (01307) 162901 🏥 (01463) 916040 🔧 (01307) 754482 🏥
(01115) 475881 🍴 (01463) 008001 🛒 (01664) 384681 🏥 (01403) 117376 ✈ (01403) 481289 ✉
(01818) 298098 🎞 (01463) 502275 🔧 (01664) 864384 🛒 (01664) 556095 ✉ (01964) 025682 🔧
(01403) 136971 🍴 (01664) 621521 🎞 (01818) 559522 Ⲁ (01964) 722321 🍴 (01635) 910925 🛒
(01700) 669434 📕 (01700) 541549 ✈ (01700) 108906 🛒 (01635) 322097 🔥 (01700) 959765 ✉
(01281) 075813 🛒 (01964) 518422 🔧 (01403) 949484 🎞 (01463) 796386 🔧 (01818) 370119 🔥
(01818) 960027 🛒 (01403) 174375 ✂ (01463) 832390 Ⲁ (01281) 299038 ✉ (01115) 886446 ✉
(01635) 300009 ✈ (01664) 343182 🔧 (01700) 336181 🚚 (01964) 777692 🔧 (01818) 164967 ✂
(01818) 819974 🚚 (01818) 290476 🔥 (01964) 532051 Ⲁ (01818) 565554 🍴 (01635) 581568 🚚
(01307) 199695 🔧 (01281) 550446 ✂ (01664) 592953 🔧 (01964) 308443 🔧 (01964) 046217 ✂
(01281) 283450 ✂ (01115) 543160 ✉ (01964) 775730 Ⲁ (01307) 602761 🎞 (01700) 039762 ✂
(01635) 327645 🏥 (01115) 552091 📕 (01281) 616806 ✈ (01635) 260244 🔧 (01964) 231215 ✉
(01307) 692957 ✂ (01403) 822731 Ⲁ (01664) 243197 📕 (01818) 053075 ✂ (01281) 405454 🛒
(01403) 219146 🚚 (01664) 644350 ✈ (01403) 617434 ✉ (01281) 711490 🔧 (01700) 364658 ✂
(01635) 303956 🔧 (01664) 620286 🔧 (01403) 095687 🔧 (01635) 865418 Ⲁ (01115) 410533 🛒
(01281) 847051 🏥 (01635) 133798 🛒 (01115) 236097 ✂ (01664) 424141 📕 (01115) 705968 🎞
(01307) 409712 🚚 (01463) 831459 🎞 (01818) 330058 🚚 (01818) 122256 🏥 (01307) 485468 ✉
(01818) 074473 🚚 (01635) 901013 🔧 (01463) 477336 🎞 (01635) 163406 🛒 (01115) 737962 🔧

Answer [   ]

QUESTION 20

Find all of the hospitals with the area code (01510)

Key

✚ Hospitals	✈ Airports	▪ Libraries	🛒 Shops	✉ Post offices	📽 Cinemas
🔥 Fire stations	🍴 Cafes	🍸 Bars	✎ Repair shops	✄ Tailors	
🚚 Shipping companies	🔧 Plumbers		

(01939) 446088 🛒 (01484) 888202 🍴 (01130) 749465 ✄ (01675) 903305 ▪ (01675) 038779 ✉
(01495) 813679 🛒 (01510) 631360 ✄ (01939) 542940 🛒 (01939) 078751 🛒 (01484) 976032 ✎
(01130) 131963 🛒 (01675) 608885 🍴 (01675) 050597 🍸 (01936) 456506 ✈ (01130) 549535 🍴
(01939) 219816 ✄ (01510) 072711 ✚ (01526) 127050 🚚 (01526) 033114 ✎ (01455) 318075 🚚
(01675) 863128 ✉ (01760) 928190 🛒 (01760) 756149 ✎ (01526) 613746 🔥 (01760) 711143 🍸
(01484) 706385 🍸 (01455) 478995 ✚ (01675) 879038 🔥 (01455) 355775 ✈ (01936) 603868 📽
(01130) 738878 ✎ (01760) 737413 🛒 (01130) 275289 ✄ (01510) 861985 📽 (01526) 543079 ▪
(01526) 262647 🍸 (01526) 308590 🛒 (01495) 879260 🚚 (01675) 865221 ✎ (01455) 130152 🚚
(01130) 492222 ✎ (01484) 567699 🚚 (01675) 363584 ✚ (01455) 852847 🍴 (01526) 562090 ✉
(01495) 637621 ▪ (01526) 525463 ✚ (01526) 422948 🛒 (01495) 847995 📽 (01455) 882352 🔥
(01510) 752676 🚚 (01675) 914884 🍴 (01936) 173989 ✎ (01526) 026024 ✄ (01675) 569583 🚚
(01455) 276433 🔥 (01510) 881505 🍸 (01760) 304346 ✎ (01760) 887178 ▪ (01495) 553433 ✚
(01675) 975300 ✎ (01510) 452421 ✚ (01455) 867182 🍴 (01510) 211655 🛒 (01526) 161634 ✚
(01526) 409316 🍸 (01675) 890609 📽 (01130) 829228 🛒 (01936) 095653 🚚 (01526) 392603 ✈
(01936) 985557 ✎ (01510) 890905 🔥 (01936) 843209 ▪ (01484) 946627 ✚ (01526) 370722 ✎
(01510) 722858 🛒 (01484) 506384 🛒 (01526) 597262 🔥 (01510) 670600 ✉ (01484) 145219 🍴
(01495) 473105 🔥 (01526) 587831 🍸 (01939) 535473 ✄ (01939) 446658 📽 (01130) 360562 ✎

Answer [   ]

TRAIN DRIVER OBSERVATIONAL ABILITY TEST – ANSWERS

1. 1

2. 1

3. 2

4. 1

5. 2

6. 2

7. 3

8. 2

9. 3

10. 2

11. 4

12. 4

13. 5

14. 3

15. 3

16. 1

17. 2

18. 2

19. 1

20. 2

CHAPTER SEVEN
SITUATIONAL JUDGEMENT TESTS

The use of Situational Judgement Tests (SJT's), sometimes known as Situational Judgement Exercises (SJE's), allow employers to gain an understanding of how a person would act in a given situation. Situational Judgement Tests are becoming increasingly popular in the recruitment process. It allows employers to gain access to a person's abilities regarding that career. They want to ensure that the person they are employing can generate a high level of performance and conduct high levels of skill and ability in an array of scenarios.

Situational Judgement Tests are often used by train operating companies in the recruitment process for Train Drivers. Train Drivers need to show the ability to act in a professional and efficient way when a particular situation requires it. They need to show high levels of understanding that, although there are many ways to react to a situation, they need to act in the best possible way to ensure safety procedures are met, maintaining professionalism and ensuring the situation is corrected in the proper manner.

Situational Judgement Tests are really simple, yet really effective. The test requires you to look at a particular situation, often reflecting a real life aspect of the job in question, and then the candidate must choose from four possible answers, the correct and most effective resolution.

There are a number of different styles regarding the Situational Judgement Test, which all test your ability to act in a specific way. The following questions are based on 'most effective'. Thus, you will be a given a situation, usually focused around the workplace, it will then give you four options to choose from. Now it is important to understand that for these tests, there are no wrong or right answers. However, employers will be able to gain an understanding of how you would react in a given situation. So, you need to choose the answer that would be 'most effective' in that situation.

For the following questions in this chapter, write the letter of the sentence that matches the course of action you would most likely take.

QUESTION 1

You are a Project Leader and manage four other team members. Two of the team members have told you they won't be able to meet the deadlines of the project. The Director of the organization reminds you the importance of meeting deadlines. Which is the most likely course of action you would take?

A. Adapt the workload for all Team Members to respect the deadlines.

B. Discuss with the two Team Members that are having difficulties, identify the causes, evaluate the remaining workload and determine an action plan to finish the project.

C. Ask the two team members that won't submit their work in time, to work additional hours in order to respect the deadlines.

D. Inform your Director of the situation. Justify the status on the project, and ask for additional resources.

Answer | B |

QUESTION 2

During your annual assessment with your Team Leader, he tells you that he considers that you could decrease your thinking time to make a decision, in order to handle more tasks.

A. Justify it with the fact that the guidelines are not always clear and that you are taking time to clarify them.

B. Justify it by saying that the complexity of the tasks required more thinking time.

C. Reduce your thinking time and spend less time dedicated to quality.

D. Keep your own way of working, but do overtime to treat more tasks.

Answer   B

QUESTION 3

You have a new Train Conductor. He is a perfectionist and pays attention to all detail. He does not hesitate to comment on the work, even when the workload is significant and the team is having difficulties to meet deadlines. This behaviour upsets you.

A. For urgent files, isolate yourself in a meeting room to work and meet the deadlines.

B. Discuss it with your Head of Unit and mention the challenges faced due to the working style of your new Train Conductor.

C. Discuss it with your Train Conductor of the challenges you are facing with his working style.

D. During the next team meeting with your Train Conductor, mention this issue and the challenges faced due his behaviour.

Answer C

QUESTION 4

One of your Team Members as a trainee train driver asks you to follow flexible working hours, as he prefers to work at night. You give your approval. However, after a couple of weeks, you noticed a decline in productivity, with delays on his projects.

A. Talk with your Team Member and explain to him that this situation cannot continue. You decide to cancel the mutual agreement.

B. Ask another Team Member of your team to manage the delayed projects.

C. Decide to absorb yourself the delayed projects.

D. Discuss it with your Team Member, inform him on your conclusions, and ask him to take a clear position on his future, so as to be able to adapt the workload of the team.

Answer | D |

QUESTION 5

With the economic crisis, the budgets of your organization have been reduced. Your Head of Unit for train drivers announces that significant changes will occur and will affect all Units. The action plan will be presented soon.

A. Continue your work normally and remain attentive to the announcements being made.

B. Talk to your colleagues to get information. Some people are always informed early of the future changes.

C. Share your concerns to your Team Leader.

D. Ask to get a meeting with management to learn of the changes before the official meeting.

Answer D

QUESTION 6

You are working on a project with two colleagues from another team. Since the beginning, the working relations have been strained. You feel as though you are constantly being criticized and that the planning of the project has been decided without you.

A. Ask to be replaced from the project.

B. Ask your Team Leader to attend the next meeting so he can see what is going on.

C. Discuss this with your colleagues by indicating to them that you are expecting better collaboration for the rest of the project.

D. Discuss this with the colleague with whom you have the best relation; mention your perception and hope for a change.

Answer $\boxed{C}$

QUESTION 7

You have been working in a team for years, with the same Team Leader. Since a couple of weeks ago, you notice that his decisions have become somewhat unreliable and questionable; his attention is low and does not seem involved with the team.

A. Discuss it with a colleague to get his views and assess together on the importance of the problem for the team.

B. Discuss it with your Team Leader and inform about your concerns.

C. Discuss it with your Head of Unit to report him the changes of your Team Leader and the impact on the team.

D. Ignore this change in the behaviour as long as it is not impacting your work directly.

Answer   B

QUESTION 8

You are working on an initiative to increase the well-being of employees, in order to reduce stress levels. Your Team Leader accused you of disclosing confidential information about the initiative to a Head of Unit. He is upset.

A. Say that agitation is useless and you want to discuss it later to justify what you did.

B. Indicate that the Head of Unit has heard about the initiative earlier from the Director and wanted to have more information.

C. Indicate that you did not have any confidentiality guidelines on the project and that a Head of Unit came to discuss about the initiative with you.

D. Apologize and make sure that it will not happen again.

Answer

QUESTION 9

A colleague of your team thinks he is always right. He does not admit his mistakes. He is considered as arrogant and self-centred. You have worked with him on tasks in the past and you did not like it. You've already told him. However, you will have to work again together on a new task.

A. Take advantage of a private talk with your colleague to inform him on the impact of his attitude and his image in the team.

B. Tell your Team Leader of the difficulties you are facing by working with your colleague, and ask for advice.

C. To work on the task, you split the tasks in order to limit the interactions with your colleague.

D. During the work, you adopt a behaviour in order to avoid discussions with your colleague.

Answer B

QUESTION 10

You are appointed coordinator for a special project that has to be completed in three months. You are very skilled for this project, while your team members assigned to the project have no experience in this area. How do you organize the work?

A. Arrange to do the maximum of the work yourself and minimize the participation of your Team Members.

B. To start with, you organize training on the skills/knowledge to have to efficiently complete the project.

C. Evaluate the strengths and weaknesses of each Team Member and assign the work based on your assessment.

D. Due to the short deadline, you ask the team to work quickly on the project and regularly monitor the progress.

Answer   B

QUESTION 11

You are Project Leader. You have established a plan and prepared the task allocation that you present to your team. For some tasks, there are no volunteers. How do you decide to allocate the work?

A. Empower your team on the importance of the project and ask them to volunteer.

B. Based on the skills of your Team Members, you decide on the best allocation.

C. Assign the work to a Team Member that already undertook similar tasks in the past.

D. Assign the work to a Team Member who has the lowest workload.

Answer A

QUESTION 12

You have been working in a team for several years. You want to evolve and get a job with more responsibilities. To get a promotion, you need to improve some skills. Your plan is to get a promotion within a few months. What are your plans?

A. Do your best to provide an excellent work during that period to get the best evaluation that can justify your promotion.

B. Discuss it with the people involved in that function to identify the skills required in order to get a promotion.

C. Discuss with your Head of Unit to assess your strengths and weaknesses. Ask to fix a training plan adapted to get the promotion.

D. You know your weaknesses and decide to follow several trainings to improve your skills.

Answer | C

QUESTION 13

You are working on a team project. During a meeting to fix the methodology, you present your plan. One of your colleagues interrupts you and challenges the validity of your plan. The rest of the group validates his plan. You are a master in that field and notice some inconsistencies in his plan. How do you react?

A. As you master well that field, you challenge the plan of your colleague. You list all inconsistencies in his plan and highlight the benefits of your plan.

B. Accept the plan of your colleague as the team has validated it. Go discuss with the Project Leader after the meeting to tell your concerns and doubts.

C. Accept the plan of your colleague as the team has validated it. Keep your plan saved to use it during the project if needed.

D. Intervene during the meeting. Tell that the plan is interesting but that you notice inconsistencies that could lead to issues later. Suggest alternatives to complete the plan.

Answer | D |

QUESTION 14

A train driver is working on an analysis for his Team Leader. He asks him to identify the correlations in some financial data so he can work on the recommendations. Following the planning, a meeting is planned at the end of the week to discuss on the results so he can already take some actions on his project. However the driver feels that it is too early and requires an additional week to finalize his analysis. How should he proceed?

A. Present the correlations that you have identified and inform him on your requirements to finalize analysis.

B. Ask you Team Leader to postpone the meeting to finalize the analysis completely.

C. Present your first conclusions but inform your Team Leader that they still need to be confirmed.

D. Go to work earlier to finalize the work before the meeting with your Team Leader.

Answer | A |

QUESTION 15

You are a Team Leader. A report presenting the activity of your team is show-ing a loss of productivity amongst train drivers. You have detected some procedures that haven't been correctly followed, leading to errors. How do you solve the issues?

A. Discuss it with other Team Leaders to know if such inconsistencies in following procedures have occurred in the past, and what was put in place to solve them.

B. Ask your superior for a performance audit to get some support in resolving these issues.

C. Organize a team meeting for train drivers, explain your findings and look for solutions together.

D. Organize a team meeting for train drivers, remind the guidelines and the importance of individual contributions to reach the objectives.

Answer | D |

QUESTION 16

An employee survey has revealed that the levels of stress is high and motivation level is very low within the organization. Your Head of Unit asks you to monitor the productivity of your team and avoid resignations, because it would penalize the organization.

- **A.** Monitor the performance and behaviour of your Team Members and assess those showing signs of stress to provide support.

- **B.** To assess the performance of your team, you organize individual meetings with each Team Member.

- **C.** During a team meeting, ask your Team Members what could be improved in their workplace to reduce the stress level.

- **D.** To maintain a good working atmosphere and cohesion, you ask a Team Member to organize a regular event outside the working hours.

Answer   C

QUESTION 17

One of your colleagues is arrogant and thinks he is the strongest person of the team. The team makes comments without his knowing. Your colleague complains to you of the cold and unfriendly atmosphere he feels in the team. He is asking you for your views.

A. Avoid the subject by saying that the atmosphere is good in the team.

B. For his own good, tell him what the other colleagues are thinking of him

C. Tell him in private what you think is the source of the problem.

D. Inform him that the reason is his behaviour towards other people.

Answer ⬚ D

QUESTION 18

You have joined a new team. Even if you have several years of experience, it is a new role for you. Your Team Leader is reviewing each file on which you are working. He is making significant changes in the recommendations before validating the file. You are frustrated that so many changes are needed. How do you react?

A. Put more energy to provide the best of yourself when working on a file and hope that the number of changes will decrease.

B. Discuss with your colleagues to see if your Team Leader has even made significant changes to their work and find out what they did about this.

C. Ask your Team Leader for feedback to show that you are determined to improve the quality of your work.

D. Ask a more experienced colleague to review some of your files before sending it to your Team Leader. And consider these learnings to improve.

Answer | C |

QUESTION 19

You are working on a project in a team. Most of your colleagues will finish their work on time. However, three of your colleagues are facing difficulties and it is generating errors. They expect to get some help to validate their work; otherwise, the quality of the project is likely to be lower. The Project Leader is often on business travel, and he asked you to supervise the work during his leave.

A. Organize an informal team meeting and establish an action plan to finalize the project by providing support to these persons.

B. Report these problems to the Project Leader to ensure that the job is being done correctly.

C. It is not your responsibilities to take initiative on this kind of issue. Continue your work.

D. Discuss it with your colleagues facing difficulties and suggest your help so they can finalize their work.

Answer | D |

QUESTION 20

Your Team Leader comes in to a train driver meeting with an aggressive attitude towards a colleague who did an error in a file. It is the first time that you see your Team Leader reacting this way in public. Your colleague tells you that he is demotivated and stressed out, and thought he did a good job.

A. Discuss the problem with your Head of Unit about the behaviour of your Team Leader and the impact on the team.

B. Avoid to make any judgment to remain outside the conflict as it does not concern you.

C. Discuss it with your colleague to check if he does not require some support in his job for specific points.

D. Inform your Team Leader about the state of your colleague and his de motivation.

Answer   C

SITUATIONAL JUDGEMENT TEST – ANSWERS

1. B
2. B
3. C
4. D
5. A
6. C
7. B
8. C
9. B
10. B
11. B
12. C
13. D
14. A
15. A
16. B
17. C
18. C
19. A
20. C

CHAPTER EIGHT

TRAIN DRIVER AWARENESS AND RECOGNITION TEST (AART)

The Train Driver Awareness and Recognition Test (AART) has been designed to allow you to measure your observational abilities and attention to detail. We have created a test to allow you to practice these key skills in order to excel your performance when you take your real assessment.

This test not only tests your attention skills, but your levels of speed, perception and visual observations, all of which are vital elements of train driving.

As part of this practice test, you will be given various images of traffic conditions. The image will be shown for approximately 1 second. You will then be asked to identify what you saw in that picture from the 5 choices listed.

For example, you may be shown a man cycling with a blue bus behind him and a tree in the background. The attention to detail in each image is key for passing the test.

You will be required to answer these questions in a quick time manner. The questions are adaptive, the change in difficulty of each image will depend on your speed and accuracy.

For the following questions in this chapter you should look at the question's image for 1 second and then note what you saw from the list of options. There may be more than one correct answer for each question, you must note them all.

It is recommended that you use a sheet of paper to cover the images in this test after you have observed them for 1 second.

QUESTION 1

What did you see in the picture?

1. A lorry

2. A train

3. A crane

4. A BMW car

5. Two way traffic

Answer [ ]

QUESTION 2

What did you see in the picture?

1. A car

2. A bus

3. A pedestrian

4. A cyclist

5. A truck

Answer [   ]

QUESTION 3

What did you see in the picture?

1. Four cars

2. A lorry

3. A road sign

4. A road junction

5. A motorcyclist

Answer ☐

QUESTION 4

What did you see in the picture?

1. A bus

2. A cyclist

3. A cyclist wearing shorts

4. Three cars

5. Two cars

Answer

QUESTION 5

How many trains did you see in the picture?

1.   1

2.   2

3.   3

4.   4

5.   5

Answer

QUESTION 6

What did you see in the picture?

1.   Motorway sign for junction 31

2.   Motorway sign for junction 30

3.   A caravan being towed

4.   A crane

5.   A lorry

Answer [   ]

QUESTION 7

What did you see in the picture?

1.   A road sign for the A429

2.   A road sign for the A449

3.   A road sign for the A229

4.   A road sign for the A228

Answer

QUESTION 8

What did you see in the picture?

1. Cycle lane

2. Traffic lights showing red

3. A bike

4. A coach

5. Bus lane

Answer [   ]

QUESTION 9

What did you see in the picture?

1. A roundabout

2. Pedestrians

3. Road signs

4. Double yellow lines

5. A bus

Answer _____

QUESTION 10

What did you see in the picture?

1. A road sign

2. A car

3. A lamppost

4. A pedestrian

5. A Vauxhall garage

Answer

QUESTION 11

What did you see in the picture?

1. Pedestrians

2. A cyclist

3. A van

4. A road sign

5. A motorbike

Answer

QUESTION 12

What did you see in the picture?

1. Car

2. Sign

3. Ship

4. Pedestrians

5. Trees

Answer

QUESTION 13

What did you see in the picture?

1. Pedestrian

2. Two cars

3. A bus

4. Two people

5. Pedestrian crossing

Answer [   ]

QUESTION 14

What did you see in the picture?

1. A cyclist

2. Bus

3. Bin

4. Bus stop sign

5. Pedestrian

Answer [   ]

QUESTION 15

What did you see in the picture?

1. A car

2. Two pedestrians

3. 3 trams

4. A van

5. A cyclist

Answer [   ]

QUESTION 16

What did you see in the picture?

1. Corner shop

2. A van

3. Cars

4. Safety barrier

5. Single yellow lines

Answer [ ]

QUESTION 17

What did you see in the picture?

1. Tree

2. A seat

3. Poster

4. 4 people

5. A bin

Answer [ ]

QUESTION 18

What did you see in the picture?

1. A tram

2. 3 pedestrians

3. Safety sign

4. 2 pedestrians

Answer

QUESTION 19

What did you see in the picture?

1. A car

2. The sea

3. Road sign

4. A cyclist

5. A pedestrian

Answer [   ]

QUESTION 20

What did you see in the picture?

1. Cars

2. Road worker

3. A cyclist

4. A bus

5. Traffic cones

Answer [   ]

AWARENESS AND RECOGNITION – ANSWERS

1. A BMW, a crane
2. A car, a cyclist
3. Four cars, a road sign, a road junction
4. A cyclist, two cars
5. 4
6. A motorway sign for junction 31, a caravan being towed, a crane, a lorry
7. A road sign for the A449
8. A cycle lane, a coach
9. A roundabout, road signs, double yellow lines
10. A car, a lamppost
11. Pedestrians, a white van
12. Car, sign, ship
13. Pedestrian, two cars, pedestrian crossing
14. Bus, bin, bus stop sign, a cyclist
15. A car, two pedestrians, a van
16. Corner shop, a van, safety barrier, cars
17. Tree, poster, a seat
18. A tram, 2 pedestrians
19. The sea, a car
20. Cars, road worker, traffic cones

You have now reached the end of the guide and we hope you have enjoyed working through the test questions.

To get more train driver tests and selection process resources you can visit **www.traindrivertests.co.uk** and get more sample train driver tests online.

Best wishes,

The how2become team

The How2become team